Harvesting the American Dream

A Memoir

———◆●◆———

From Farm to Classroom:
The Spruill Journey

By Harrell S. Spruill

D1213446

Note for Librarians: A cataloguing record for this book is available from Library and Archives
Canada at www.collectionscanada.ca/amicus/index-e.html
ISBN 1-4120-8199-8

Printed in Victoria, BC, Canada. Printed on paper with minimum 30% recycled fibre.
Trafford's print shop runs on "green energy" from solar, wind and other environmentally-friendly power sources.

TRAFFORD
PUBLISHING™
Offices in Canada, USA, Ireland and UK

Book sales for North America and international:
Trafford Publishing, 6E–2333 Government St.,
Victoria, BC V8T 4P4 CANADA
phone 250 383 6864 (toll-free 1 888 232 4444)
fax 250 383 6804; email to orders@trafford.com
Book sales in Europe:
Trafford Publishing (UK) Limited, 9 Park End Street, 2nd Floor
Oxford, UK OX1 1HH UNITED KINGDOM
phone 44 (0)1865 722 113 (local rate 0845 230 9601)
facsimile 44 (0)1865 722 868; info.uk@trafford.com
Order online at:
trafford.com/05-3165

10   9   8   7   6   5   4   3

Dedication

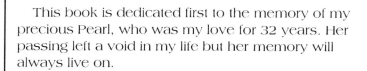

This book is dedicated first to the memory of my precious Pearl, who was my love for 32 years. Her passing left a void in my life but her memory will always live on.

I thank my butterfly, Annetta Spruill, for being a supportive, kind, and caring wife. She accepted my children as if they were her own and has given unselfishly to them and my grandchildren.

I hope that my son and daughter, Kevin Spruill and Kecia Spruill Johnson, as well as my grandchildren, will treasure this story of their ancestors and understand why I raised them as I did.

Two good friends and advisors helped make my success possible. Without John Prann's knowledge and loans, I would never have been able to buy my land. I miss his wisdom and hope to see him on the other side. My attorney, Michael Roblyer, has provided me with wonderful advice over many years. I recall going to a County Council zoning meeting in the late 1960s where I overheard people wondering why a white man would represent me. Times changed, but his excellent legal counsel has remained the same to this day.

Finally, I dedicate this story to my Spruill siblings. I will always treasure my relationship with my brothers and sisters. We have a lot for which to be grateful. Although we came into the world with underclass status, through the grace of God we excelled in every endeavor to which we aspired.

Contents

—◆●◆—

Preface

The Spruill Journey

———————◆●◆———————

At the ragged edge of a little field several miles outside the tiny town of Travis, North Carolina, you can still find the remains of my father's barn. The tin roof has collapsed onto the weathered timbers, and the loblolly pines have sprouted around it. Stand next to the ruins, look out toward the road, and you can see the entire 13 acres that were Solomon Spruill's domain. The farmhouse still stands where my mother fed and clothed the family, and provided the driving force for the education of her nine children. (A tenth child died as a baby.) From these few acres, my father carved out a living for himself and his large family. In a time and region of the country where blacks owned almost nothing, Solomon proudly ruled over his postage-stamp-sized kingdom.

This humble place of dirt roads and outdoor toilets was the beginning of the journey for my Spruill brothers and sisters. For all of us, that dusty dirt road led to at least a high school degree, a rare enough accomplishment in those days. Some of us went even further to earn teaching degrees and college diplomas. Two went to graduate school. From an underclass, impoverished, minority status we became educators, school principals, and even the dean of a graduate school.

I write this memoir to document our journey from farm to classroom. I want to share some of the principles that I believe led to our success and that have led to the success of so many other blacks in the community. The first part of the book details life growing up on the farm with brothers and sisters closest to my age. The second part relates my life in education and my attempts to create charitable organizations that would bring some of the important lessons of that farm to modern children.

Rising in society is very difficult, if not impossible, without the help and direction of parents. Not only did my father provide the family with food, clothing, and shelter through difficult times, he provided an example of the kind of work ethic required to achieve any goal. My mother focused on our education, encouraging, inspiring, prodding, and disciplining us. It was simply not an option to stop our studies before we earned a high school degree. Children will not naturally see the value of an education unless it is drilled into them by their parents. Nobody else will make sure children attend and respect their school, and nobody else will pick up children after they falter, and insist that they try again.

My mother always spoke of education as the key to escaping both poverty and the system of racial injustice in the United States at the time. Only through education could black people change their lives for the better. The country has changed since then, but my mother's philosophy is still absolutely true. The only way forward out of poverty and injustice is through education. Back then, a high school degree was the basic level of education. Now a college degree is essential. I don't see enough emphasis on doing whatever it takes to get a child down that long road to a college diploma. We don't view it with the high regard due to a golden key to a better life.

The final element in the Spruill journey is the accumulation of wealth and ownership through planning and hard work, and a legacy being left to both children and the community. Too often I see a lack of long-range planning in the black community. A day-to-day philosophy and lifestyle, which is understandably prevalent in impoverished communities, mostly prevails. We must rise above these constraints and work toward investment in land and business that will grow in the future. We must allow our children to start their lives with more resources and money than we had to begin our lives. All that I will leave behind to my own children and the community comes from an investment in land. Buying the land and owning it over the years meant decades of hard work, but it paid off in the end. We must do more to promote minority ownership.

The Spruill journey mirrors many other journeys made by blacks of my generation, up from poverty and institutionalized racism to education and prosperity. It is a journey that is still important, even in these days of expanded opportunities for minorities. I hope our story will provide inspiration and light along that path.

Chapter 1

The Farm

———◆●◆———

When I was a small boy, my father entrusted me with a great deal of responsibility on his farm in Travis, North Carolina. Out of his nine children, perhaps he felt that I would follow his ways because he had given me his name, Solomon, as my middle name. Solomon Spruill believed in God and the Baptist Church, but above all he believed in work, most of it difficult and physical, and done in all kinds of weather the year round. Perhaps he thought that his namesake would believe the same, even as a child.

My father never said much to me until I was around three years old, when he decided I was old enough to start helping him. My mother was the talkative parent, the one who told me stories and cooed at me and paid attention when I cried. She was the one who laughed when I climbed inside my father's work shoes and clomped around the house. I was so small all you could see was the shoes and my head peeking out the top. After that, she always called me Boots. I didn't have much to do with my father because he was always out on the farm and had little time or talk for young children.

1

He could talk religious if he felt like it, and he would say an eloquent Sunday prayer. But most of the time that I knew him, he kept his words and thoughts to himself.

When I was three, however, he came into breakfast after his early chores and told me it was time I started to work in the fields with him. My older brother and sisters that lived at home had already finished their chores and walked to school. "We're going to go out there and plow cotton this morning, and I want you to follow behind me and uncover the plants," he said. Solomon's farm was only 13 acres but he farmed it as if he owned 50 acres. He was a very progressive farmer and very proud of his land. Every inch of it was used to make money or produce food for the family and livestock.

After we finished breakfast, my mother put my little straw hat on my head, made sure my overalls were fastened, and sent me out after my father. I toddled behind him to the barn, trying to keep up with his long strides. I learned quickly that my father expected me to keep up with him and work like a man, though I was barely out of diapers. All of Solomon's children were expected to do the same, and he was quick with his hands if the work was not done properly, efficiently, and

Georgiana W. Spruill, age 18

without complaint. Above all, he did not tolerate complaining.

In the area of North Carolina where the Spruills had their farms, outside the village of Travis and near the sea, farmers worked on either sandy or clay soil. Those with sandy soil used horses to pull the plow through the earth, and those with clay soil, such as my father, drove mules.

Laura and Cora were our two mules as I was growing up. My father never bought mules that someone else had used. He didn't trust another man's training when it came to mules. Laura was an old beast even when I was a child. The family used her mostly to hitch to our cart and drive to school and church when the weather was bad. Cora was young and fast, and she never obeyed anybody but my father. Some mornings she let herself be led out of her stall sweetly, submitting quietly to the hitching of the plow. Other mornings she simply refused, kicking at my father with her hind legs and braying with displeasure. My father would beat her with a long leather strap until she obeyed. It terrified me to see her kicking and braying so loud it hurt my ears, and to hear the snap of that leather on her hide. She never got my father once, though. He knew what he was doing with a mule. Eventually she would have enough of getting beat and come out to go to work.

The plow was a steel blade hooked to an oak board. This board was then attached to a swinger tree with two handles for driving, and the whole thing harnessed to the mule. My father would hold the handles, get the mule moving, and walk behind as the mule dragged the blade through the earth. Solomon kept the furrow straight and at a level depth. He plowed between the rows of growing

3

plants, turning the soil over to bring fresh dirt to the roots of the plants.

I quickly found that my job was to walk behind him and clear the dirt that spilled from the blade, sometimes covering the green sprouts of the young corn or cotton. I would bend over and brush the dirt gently with my hands, being careful not to damage the plant. We would go up one row and down the other until the entire field was plowed.

My father never seemed to be affected by the humid heat that blanketed North Carolina in the spring and summer, even in the fields where we had no protection from the harsh sun. Beneath his blue denim overalls, my father always wore old-fashioned red long underwear that buttoned up the front, no matter the heat of the day. He claimed winds blowing over his sweaty skin cooled him. He kept his hair short under his straw hat. I would stand in the door of his bedroom and watch him trim it himself with scissors and a razor, using the same careful, competent motions with which he did everything around the farm. He had the long, lean muscles of a man who works his body from sunrise to sunset for years on end.

As we made our way down the rows at a stately pace, I watched my father behind the plow, holding the handles steady, a constant effort to keep the blade true at the proper depth. He was a tall figure against a clear blue sky, trodding slowly in worn boots behind the mule. He would turn to check me from time to time to make sure I was working right behind him. If something was wrong, he would tell me to fix it. Otherwise we worked for hours without saying a word.

The sun rose higher in that cloudless Southern sky, bringing with it a heat that thickened the air and felt like a tangible presence against the skin. I kept to a good pace, dusting the plants without hurting the shoots. When I stopped to look up from my task, I could see the line of tangled pine forest bordering our fields, our blue house and livestock yard, and in the distance my grandfather's house on his land. Beyond that house lay my uncle's farm. That was as far as I knew the world went, these 50 acres farmed by three Spruills, and the dirt road that ran between them. But mostly I kept my head down and hands moving.

By noon we had finished the plowing, but I had other chores to complete before my brothers and sisters got home from school. My father headed off to the barn without a word, a single glance reminding me to keep working. As long as the sun was up, there was work to do on the farm.

In the late 1920s, and especially in that part of the country, very few blacks owned land for farming or otherwise. Many of the black families that I knew relied on hiring themselves out to pick cotton, potatoes, peanuts, or other crops. They also would find work hoeing the weeds out of soil reserved for field peas or green beans. The land was mostly owned by whites, particularly huge farms of hundreds of acres on the other side of the city of Columbia, which everybody called "The Plantations."

The Spruills, however, were the exception. I never discovered how my grandfather laid hands on his 50 acres. It was an unusual possession for a man whose parents had been held as slaves in the same state. When my father came of age, he bought 13 acres from my grandfather for $400. My grandfather believed that giving children anything more than shelter and food spoiled them insufferably, a parenting philosophy that my father retained for his children. He worked for years to pay my grandfather that $400. My mother called his land "Solomon's Castle," and he ran it as such.

The whites in the local community seemed to respect my father because he owned land and got so much from so small a parcel. When he went into the drugstore in Columbia, I remember that he used the front door instead of the back door reserved for the "colored." Later in his life, some whites tried unsuccessfully to help him buy the 40 acres adjacent to his farm, apparently because they were concerned that someone who knew nothing about farming would get a hold of it. He worked on the road crew in the winter, paving and grading, so the whites knew him and seemed to respect his efforts.

Solomon's Castle, however, came with a price. The whole family worked constantly to keep it running, resting only on Sundays. By the time I came along, four children had already grown up and moved on. During my time on the farm, the Spruill household consisted of my older brother Elijah, older sisters, Von and Eva, and the baby, Albert.

We lived in an area called the Back Road, after the dirt road, dusty in summer and muddy in winter, that

The Back Road

traveled east from the village of Travis toward the swamp and the ocean. Travis wasn't much—a country village with a general store and a service station, a mill to grind corn into meal, a few rows of small houses. Everyone had to go to Columbia, about six miles further on a real blacktop highway, to get clothing and supplies. Although it was still just a small town built around the fish and potato-grating industry, with some saw mills and logging around its fringes, Columbia seemed like the big city to us.

The Back Road was isolated and wholly rural. You could walk a mile or two between farmhouses. Because we were so far out, my mother ordered the children's clothing from the pages of the Sears Roebuck catalog, mainly overalls with patches on the knees or steel-plated brogans. She had our Sunday suits hand-made by traveling salesmen. My younger brother Al and I called these suits our "Revolutionary clothes" because they looked like something little boys would have worn in the Colonial days we read about in school, with George Washington" knickers and frilly collars.

The farther you walked down the Back Road, the swampier it got. The Spruill farms were fairly dry with clay soil, but the soil got sandier closer to the ocean. On either side of the road were stands of thick pine trees and shadowy undergrowth, untouched forest broken at long intervals by fields or front yard. All the roads were similar, dirty and dusty with ruts from carts and trucks, lonely even in sunlight and quite frightening by night. All kinds of animals lived in the woods. I had heard that bears prowled the forests, and the thought of their teeth and claws kept me scared for many years.

I was five years old when I first confronted the dirt road alone. When my great aunt passed way, my father asked me to walk to get a death certificate at the post office, which was a farmer's house. The shortest way was down the Back Road and then along a little-used track through deep forest on either side. I left at six in the

Cornfield

morning and hiked the whole way in the dead center of the road, fearful that an animal would leap from the woods to eat me. I didn't get home until two in the afternoon, just in time for the funeral. The white undertaker was waiting for the death certificate with his motorcar hearse to carry the coffin. The mules and carts of our relatives and neighbors lined up behind the car in a precise order depending on their relationship to the deceased. The hearse set off at an easy pace, allowing the mules to keep up. I was also scared of the cemetery where we were headed, but I felt tremendously relieved to be back among my family after the lonely journey.

The Back Road was pretty well mixed, black and white. Regardless of color, its residents shared the same predicament: farming was the only option to make a living, whether you owned land or worked as hired labor on someone's farm. Women and children worked alongside the men, pulling the grass out of the field, hoeing weeds, or harvesting crops. My mother was an exception because my father rarely permitted her to work outside the house, even on the farm. Only at the cotton harvest did she come into the fields. The black schools held back the start of classes until October to allow children to pick cotton, which was a primary source of income for many families.

We were lucky enough to have our 13 acres, but with an acre devoted to the house and a yard for livestock, my father had to rotate the crops every year and think creatively to get three different crops in the field each season. In April, the feed corn went in, followed a few weeks later by the cotton. In September, after the corn had been plowed for the last time, he planted soybeans between the rows of corn.

By August, the corn was dry enough to pull the leaves as fodder for the animals during the winter. On the hottest day in the first or second week of the hottest month, we would cut the leaves from the corn plants and tie them to the stalks for drying. The oppressive heat made it a sweaty, dizzying job that seemed to last forever, but it also cured the fodder quickly. After a few days of curing, we harvested the fodder by tying three or four of the small bundles into one big bundle. In the end, we stored about a thousand big bundles in the barn to feed the mule and cows without having to grow grain for feed. In this way, my father was able to use every inch of his land for profit.

The cotton harvest came in September. The whole family went to the field to get the crop in. I remember working alongside my mother, who had balanced baby Al on top of her cotton sack so she could keep an eye on him while she worked. My father also hired one or two

Harrell's mother Georgiana Spruill, Albert Westley Spruill, his wife, Dee (Floydelia) Spruill, and Harrell's sister, Vonbeulah Spruill.

Family Members (brothers and sisters) at a Family Reunion in July 1983.

outside workers to help because picking cotton was difficult and time-consuming. You had to pry open the prickly cotton bur and extract the wad of cotton. It took a skilled hand.

The corn came down in October. It wasn't sweet corn for the table but a dried corn that fed the livestock or went to the mill to be ground and sold. With just the soybeans left in the field, we would wait for the first killing frost. The next day, we would break the soybeans from the vine and pile them in the barn. On a windy fall day, with the chilly wind blowing through the barn, we spread the beans on a canvas and beat them with a pole until the beans broke from the pods. The wind whipped around and blew off the debris, and then we could sweep the beans into a bin, ready to be sold.

This process of planting, cultivating, and harvesting continued every year. Nobody had tractors or automated equipment at that time. On Saturdays, we spent the morning shelling corn off the cob by hand until we had two or three bushels to take to the mill to be ground into meal. Huge loads of crops were transported from one side of the farm to the other on mules. The simplest tasks required large amounts of physical labor.

In addition to the difficulty of farming, many in the black community of Travis went hungry or lived in great poverty, particularly during the Depression. We never suffered in such ways, largely because my father never relented in his work. It is hard to say whether my father's intensity and unforgiving work ethic made him success-ful, or whether it was the harsh conditions of the farm that made him so intense and often unforgiving. Regard-less, he was focused on the business of making the farm work at every minute of every hour. He expected and demanded the other members of the Spruill family to do the same.

A Family Reunion at Harrell's home.

Enjoying good company and good food at Von's home during the Spruill Reunion.

Chapter 2

Summer and Winter

—————◆●◆—————

I was about five years old when Laura the old mule passed away. I was a country child, and so I feared the spirits and devils that seemed to teem in those dark woods and quiet fields under the light of the moon. I had seen Laura's dead body, and I greatly feared her ghost haunting the farm and the house, a fact that my mother used to her advantage. I would quickly stop misbehaving if threatened with a visit from Old Laura's four-legged ghost.

"If you don't go right to sleep, Old Laura is going to get you," my mother told me, and I raced down the dark hall into the pitch-black bedroom. I quickly threw off my overalls and slid under the sheets next to my brother Al. We didn't have any special pajamas. We just slept right in the same underwear we wore all day.

Because of my fearful nature, I was happy to share the same bed and room with Albert and Elijah. Elijah was six years older than I was and probably didn't feel the same way. But Al and I figured that the more people around, the less the chance of being visited by haunts. Elijah could stay out late, so we sometimes had to wait several hours after going to bed until he came in and made us feel safe.

I lay there shivering, listening to Al breathe, wondering if he was asleep. To my dismay, I had to use the bathroom. Because our outhouse was kept down in the woods, away from the house, I always tried to take care of my business before it got dark. I had to tiptoe down the hall to the back door. There was no chance of my going down to the woods at this hour. Even the adults rarely did so. They were more scared of the snakes in the bushes than ghosts. I was scared of both, so I raced out through the yard to the edge of the cotton, keeping my eyes wide open, trying to look every which way at once for spooks that might be coming my way. I went as quickly as possible, feeling extremely vulnerable out there with my pants down. In the lamp-lit days before light pollution, an innumerable amount of stars literally dusted the sky. I could see no sign of humanity except our little house among the fields. I sprinted back to the safety of my bed. Despite my fears, I fell asleep quickly because the farm wore me out every day. When the sun rose, so would the family, to begin another day of work.

The smell of my mother's hot biscuits and ham cooking in the kitchen woke me just at dawn. At that time, the kitchen was a separate building from the main house, accessible by a raised walkway out the back door. I roused Al, washed my face and hands with soap and water from a metal pan, and rushed into the kitchen. My sisters Eva and Von came downstairs from the room they shared, and all of us ate together. After a prayer, we wolfed down my mother's delicious breakfast and the boys ran out into the fields to join my father.

According to a parenting philosophy established long before I was born, the girls didn't work in the fields with the boys. They did, however, have their own chores to do outside the house, as well as helping my mother with the cooking and cleaning. Von and Eva toiled with us in the garden on the side of the house, raising cabbage, kale, lima beans, string beans, tomatoes, and watermelon for our table. They were responsible for pulling bugs off the greens and cabbages and sealing them in jars to die. They also prepared fresh straw for the cow and mule stalls in the barn.

Al and I went straight for the barn to get the cows out of the stalls. Of course, we had to wrestle to see which cow we would get. We settled every question by wrestling, all the way from elementary to high school. At first I could always get what I wanted because he was so much smaller, but as we got older more and more matches ended in a draw, which didn't decide anything. Once we got the matter settled of who had to take care of which milk cow, we put them on chains and led them out to the road. Our little fenced-in yard around the house wouldn't grow grass because of all the animals running around on it all day long. Chickens, geese, ducks, dogs, and cats all roamed that one acre of land. The milk cow had to be fed with the wild grass and plants growing wild along the dirt road.

We both hated this chore more than any other. The cows had to be kept on chains while they fed or they would get into the neighbor's fields, or worse, trample my father's crops. It took several hours for a cow to eat, with nothing to do but follow it around and make sure it didn't get in trouble. Kids would walk by on the road, on their way to go swimming or have fun, and they would tease us for having to stand around all morning holding a cow. I would ignore them, but Al, with his quick temper, would sometimes get in fights in the dust. Time rarely passes so slowly as on a hot day in the country with nothing to do but hold onto a chain while a cow slowly grazes its way to a full stomach. With other chores, Al and I could invent games and keep each other company, but we had to graze our cows apart from each other.

At the end of this chore, we raced happily to gather eggs from under the house before lunch. Our frame house was built on cement blocks about two feet off the ground, as was common in the area. My father and some other men constructed it a few years before I was born. The pine siding was painted blue and always kept fresh and neat. The porch on the front of the house was screened so we could sit outside on summer evenings.

Some people closed up the space beneath their house with boards or bricks, but my father used the space for the chickens to lay their eggs. They also laid them in the weeds under the barn. We got baskets and went around the edges searching for eggs. With that complete, we wrestled to see who would have to crawl underneath. Rats, snakes, and mice hid in the shade and made their nests. Al had to shimmy underneath, hating every minute he was under there.

We took advantage of every little minute of free time we had. We played horseshoes, built our own rag baseballs wrapped with twine strings and played with flat baseball bats. One time we sold enough seeds from a company to get a basketball as a prize and made our own goal in the barn. Al was my closest friend and confidant, especially in the summer. Elijah was too old to play with us, and the girls were kept mainly in the house. We were out of doors all day, trying to find the fun in work, sharing secrets, splitting our chores, and growing up together.

In winter, the farm was like a different world. On rising, I put on my clothes as quickly as possible. The air was freezing in our room because the only heat source in the house was the stove in the living room. My overalls were stiff after being left out all night. As I crossed the uncovered walkway to the kitchen, I saw snow blowing across the open fields. The pines along the line of forest were bent low with ice on their branches. It was a relief to get into the hot kitchen, warmed by the stove, filled with delicious smells from the cooktop.

"Before you sit down, Boots, go on and unfreeze the pump," my mother asked. I grumbled, but grabbed the bucket of boiling water from the top of the stove. I hauled it about fifty yards to the pump, holding it steady at the end of my straight arm, being careful not to spill the sloshing water on my legs. Drops splashed out and steamed when they hit snow. I carefully raised the bucket over the top of the pump and poured it on the ice-locked metal. I quickly grabbed one of the buckets sitting by the pump and with some effort got the handle moving up and down, sending a trickle of water into the bucket. Eventually, I got two buckets full and hauled them, struggling, into the kitchen.

I decided to do my chores before breakfast. My main winter task was to keep the two stoves in the house supplied with enough fuel to keep the fires burning and the house heated. The supply of logs on the front porch was running low so I made several trips to the woodpile to resupply the stacks. The big logs were already split, but I had to chop up pine branches for kindling and make sure I had enough small chips that would easily burn.

I stomped the snow from my boots and went into the living room. The steel stove was meant to provide heat for the whole house. We couldn't afford cast iron, so the steel buckled under use and we had to buy a new one every year. It was about three feet around and three feet high. The stove was held off the floor by legs and a metal plate underneath caught errant ashes or embers that otherwise would have burned through the pine floor. I used a shovel to clean out the old ashes and built a new fire. The ashes were kept in a bucket and spread on the soil of the farm as a fertilizer. Nothing went to waste.

After breakfast, I began my journey to elementary school with Al, Von, and Eva. Elijah was already at the high school. It was a walk of about three miles down the Front Road toward Travis. No school bus came around for the black schoolchildren attending the Tyrell County Training School.

We attended school every day, no matter the weather or chores left to do on the farm. My mother and father shared the belief that education was the way upward for black people in America. Thus, he allowed us to leave the farm to go to school.

My mother, however, was the driving force behind the education of the Spruill children. She had gone only as far as eighth grade, but she enjoyed reading and learned to do so well. She believed that truth could be found in the written word, whether it was our storybooks or the pages of her much-worn Bible. She insisted we attend class, and she checked our schoolwork and praised us for our grades. She was a heavy woman, but she would leave her many duties behind and walk three miles to our school on many occasions to attend PTA meetings, children's program, plays, and performances. My mother never dressed flashy and she always had her hair pulled back in a ball. Nobody in Travis got their hair done anyway. Everybody cut it at home. Nothing interested her more than her children's success in school, which to her meant they would be successful in life. She had already put four poor black children through high school and had two children in college. She was determined that her remaining five would also get a higher education.

The long dirt drive from our house to the road was treacherous with ice and banks of crusted snow. The wind whipped at our legs and pushed us about, but the snow had stopped and the clouds were clearing. It would be another bright, cold day. The temperature biting at my nose told me that soon my father would call on a few of his neighbors and slaughter the eight or so hogs we put up for food every winter. I disliked the slaughter, the blood, and the disturbing sound the pigs made as their throats were cut. I had slopped these pigs and cared for them throughout the year. But I knew, as all farmboys do, that their death was necessary for the survival the family and farm. Their meat sustained us and we used their fat to make grease or soap.

My father would lead the pig to an area by the woodpile and with one smooth motion cut its throat with a sharp knife. As he led the bleeding pig to the woodpile, the animal would fall over and die from loss of blood. If it somehow survived all the way to the woodpile, one of

17

my father's friends would kill it with an axe to the top of the head.

Once a pig was dead, my father dashed the body immediately with boiling water and the skin was scraped with blades to remove the hairs. If the water and the body cooled, it became impossible to remove the hairs. My mother and her friends would try to have a good time despite their dirty, gruesome job, talking and laughing with each other as they cleaned the intestines. Everyone who helped got a portion of the meat, and we always gave some meat to the poor people in the community. Charity was always present in the black community of Travis, and as poor as we were, some people suffered from poverty more than we did.

My thoughts of the coming slaughter were interrupted by the bitter wind threatening to blow Al right off the road into the ditch. I wished my father had suggested that he drive us in the mule cart, as he did some occasions when the weather was bad. Without snow, however, we were on our own.

At least in winter all the kids walking to school kept to themselves, bundled up beneath coats and homemade scarves, too cold to mess with each other. In the spring I had been pestered by a bully who tried to pick a fight with me every day on the way home. I didn't like to fight, but he insisted. Finally we wrestled and I ended up beating him. I guess he didn't know that I wrestled my brothers every chance I got. His defeat, however, didn't deter him. The next day he threatened and pushed me all the way home. I knew where he lived, so I told my mother what had been happening. She said she'd take care of it. A few days later, he ran up from behind and whacked me in the head with a tree branch. He was suspended for a week and, after that, thankfully left me alone.

The elementary schoolhouse was a seven-room building stuck in the middle of the forest with a playground out back. Each grade had its own classroom where a teacher taught all the subjects. Fifteen or 20 kids sat in chairs without desks. It wasn't until the upper school that we actually had desks. The rooms were heated by coal-burning stoves. We sat at attention in the warm room, trying to learn and stay awake, while outside the wind blew. In my second-grade class, I excelled at mathematics and science, but I struggled with English, particularly spelling. My struggles in this subject would continue for years.

When I was excused to use the restroom, I ran out the front door to the woods across the road. The outdoor toilets in the back of the school were not well kept, and most children didn't dare go near them.

At noon we ate lunch and were released into the snowy yard for recess. In warm weather, I would play endless hours of baseball on the school's diamond. In winter, however, we just ran around and tried to stay warm. Sometimes we just played on the school stage. When I got thirsty, I went to the pump and used my cupped hand to sip water so cold it made my teeth hurt.

Community Center built on the property of the Old Travis Elementary School that was burned to the ground by a hate group. Standing in front of the building are Harrell Spruill and his brother-in-law, Anthony Jordan.

After school all the children went into the forest to rake up pine needles and leaves. Every day we piled up huge mounds of dirt and leaves that my father would use in the spring as a fertilizer. I know he made us rake partly to keep us busy in those months outside the growing season, but the dirt and leaves also served as an effective compost.

Most nights in the winter, the family gathered around the stove in the living room after dinner. My mother would read out loud to us. Enoch Arden and the miser Silas Marner became living characters to me, as real as the living. Sometimes I feared they would be waiting for me when I went down the dark hall to bed. We huddled about the stove on our wooden chairs, in the light of a lamp, listening to my mother's voice tell us the Bible stories of Sampson and Delilah, David, Joseph, John the Baptist, and the Babe of Bethlehem. As the stories ended, my father would explain their lessons and lead us in a discussion of their meaning for the faithful.

On this winter night, however, my mother intended to drill me in spelling yet again. My second-grade teacher, who was also my first cousin and had a soft spot for my troubles, had come by earlier to tell my mother that if I didn't improve my spelling and pass the exam, I would be held back for another year. She pleaded with my mother to get me to pass that exam. Hearing this, my mother of course took charge and began drilling me in spelling every night around the kitchen table. She would read a word and I would have to spell it. I got tired of working on it, but the night before the test my mother was not about to let me go into the living room with my siblings and relax.

Spelling just did not come naturally to me, but I wanted to make my mother proud and spare her the shame of having a Spruill child held back a grade. I had tried my hardest for several weeks, but the night before the test I just wasn't focusing. I wanted to be off playing with Al. I kept misspelling words until my mother, in great frustration, whacked me over the head with the spelling primer and sent me to bed crying. I suspect she cried some tears of worry that night as well.

The next morning I shuffled off to school, trying to figure out a way to get out of this exam. I didn't want to be a failure, but I knew there was no way I could spell all those words. I sat in my chair all morning feeling sick. When it came time for the test, however, I knew almost every word on it. My mother had drilled me so hard that I had actually become a good speller. Not only did I not get held back, but I made the spelling team. It was one of the first of many experiences with the truth that hard work pays off. With improved grades in English, and my stellar performance in math and science, in a few years I skipped the seventh grade and went straight to the eighth grade, which at that time was the first year of high school.

My mother always met us out on the porch when we came home from school, and she was delighted when I passed the spelling exam, wrapping me up in a big hug. She was also proud as could be when I skipped a grade. But I have no doubt that if I had failed that exam she would have been waiting for me out in front of the house as always, excited to see me, ready to give me a hug and make me feel that I would succeed the next time.

Chapter 3

The Plantations

————————◆●◆————————

My mother shook me from a deep sleep, moving around the bed to wake my brothers. She lit the lamp and left the room to pack our lunches. My brothers and I sleepily pulled on our overalls and boots, and stumbled into the kitchen for breakfast. Von and Eva were already eating. We took our lunches and went out to the dirt road to wait for the truck that would pick us up. The sky had begun to glow along the treetops, but the sun was not yet up.

When Spruill children reached the age of six or seven, they began to earn their living off the farm. In June and July, we were hired out to dig white potatoes on the massive farms on the other side of Columbia. Many different whites owned property there, but they were universally called "The Plantations" by the blacks of Travis. The money we made went to my mother to pay for our clothes, books, and school supplies. Rather than resent having to work for a living so early in life, the children looked forward to this opportunity to get off the farm and out from under my father's judging eye and quick hand. It was actually easier toiling in a white man's fields than on my father's farm.

Elijah, however, sometimes didn't go to work. He would come out to the road with us as if he was going to go, then take off to spend the day on his own. He did what he wanted to do, and taking a beating didn't seem to deter him. He was the only child who dared ignore what my father told him to do. Though my mother

pleaded with him to behave, she would give him cash so
that my father would not find out that he had skipped
work.

A large open-back truck came over the rise, bump-
ing along the rutted road, and we lined up to climb
aboard. We joined black people of all ages sitting on the
wood slats, from children like us to women without many
teeth. Those who had no land looked forward to this time
of the year when steady money for a few weeks meant
they ate regularly and could buy a few things to hold
them until the next crop harvest.

The trucks drove us west, past Columbia, stopping
every now and then for a worker to climb into the back.
When about 30 of us were packed in, we jostled our way
to a farm where acres on acres of white potatoes were
waiting to be harvested.

We arrived as the sun finally came up, and we
spilled out into the fields. The crew chief waited for us, a
white man who assigned us where to start picking. The
Spruills stuck together, taking rows next to each other.

I began my row at one end of the field, the other end
so far away I could hardly see it. Because the boss paid
10 cents per barrel, I learned quickly how to work fast
and efficiently. I leaned over and grabbed the potato vine,
ripping it from the ground. I shook the vine violently from
side to side, knocking clumps of dirt and potatoes to the
ground, and then moved to the next vine. All around me,
the workers were doing the same thing, silently and
intently. We all knew that the amount of cash we took
home on Friday depended on how hard we worked each
minute in the field, so there was little talk or idle chatter.
Any opportunity to make money was treated seriously.

When I reached the end of the row, I grabbed two
buckets and began working my way back, picking up the
potatoes I had shaken off the vine and dropping them
into one of my buckets according to size: large or small.

When my buckets were full, I carried them to one of two large barrels marked by size and dumped them. The Spruills combined their efforts in filling the barrels, and when one was full, the men in charge marked it in their ledger by our names and took the barrel away.

We worked through the morning with hardly a word. About noon, everybody stopped for 10 or 15 minutes for lunch. We had sandwiches from home, crackers, maybe sardines if we were lucky. In those days, our meals consisted of pork, pork, and more pork. Sometimes this pattern would be interrupted with a chicken from the yard. I ate my lunch quickly, sitting close to my siblings, then stuck my head under the pump to cool off.

The afternoon was the same as the morning except hotter, shaking the potato from the vine, collecting and sorting. When the sun started to set, it was time to climb on the truck and get home. The workers were paid on Friday evenings. The workers were expected to keep records of how many barrels they filled to match with the owner's ledger. The foreman sat at a table, checking his records, and paid out of a stack of cash.

The rocking of the truck on the road and the exhaustion of the day made us sleepy on the ride home. One by one, the workers climbed down at their houses or shacks, until there were just a few of us left, silently rocking and riding under the open night sky. When we reached our house, we jumped down and went down the long drive, through fields on either side to our house. The lamps were on, glowing in the windows, and we knew that my mother had a hot meal waiting on the stove.

Regaining our energy, we rushed in to wash the caked soil from our hands and arms. My mother had water ready in wash pans, a fresh cloth for scrubbing. We threw the dirty water into the yard. As we ate our meal, our mother kept us company, asking us questions and telling us stories.

Harrell Spruill and brother-in-law Anthony Jordan, standing in front of torn down structure of familly home in Travis, North Carollina.

Eating in the light of the kerosene lamp, listening to her voice, I felt safe and tired. I enjoyed going out to work, away from my father and the grind of the farm. I liked it when they handed us the cash money from my labor, and knowing that my mother would keep it safe for the things I needed for school. When we were done eating, there was no time for stories in the living room. We had only a few hours to sleep before we would be awakened again to go out to the plantations. Al and I went down the dark hall to our room, took off our dirty clothes, curled up, and went quickly to sleep.

Chapter 4

Sunday

Work and school was the rule from Monday to Saturday, sunup to sundown, but on Sunday the Spruill family rested. Resting, of course, meant putting on our finest clothes and gathering for prayer and religious study, first in the living room of our house and then at the Baptist church. My parents both came from religious families and the church lay at the core of everything that happened in the black community.

Al, Elijah, and I wore our store-bought suits with ready-made ties that clipped under the collar of our shirts. We had special caps that we wore only on Sundays. Eva and Von came downstairs in dresses sewn by

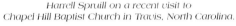

Harrell Spruill on a recent visit to Chapel Hill Baptist Church in Travis, North Carolina.

my mother and one of her friends. Their hair was done up nice, and all the women wore Sunday hats, the bigger and wider the better.

After breakfast, we knelt in a circle in the living room while my father led us in prayer. He made sure Al was close to hand, for he tended to fidget and grow bored during this time. Al was an independent, curious child from an early age.

With Al right next to my father, we recited the Lord's Prayer out loud. I had my eyes closed, listening to the sound of those familiar voices reciting those well-known, comforting words. I remembered when I had been baptized into the Baptist church, riding in a caravan of carts from the church to the river, about five miles away. Everyone gathered along the bank in their finest clothes, singing songs and praising the Lord. Those to be baptized changed into white robes and

were led into the river. The minister said a few words, pushed me down under the cool water, and when I came up, I was a member of the church. I had no special religious feelings. I believed in the teachings of the church, and I felt comfortable following the traditions of my parents. For the congregation, baptizing was one of the happiest days of the year because they believed that their own sins were being washed away along with those being baptized. Everyone came to the river to get clean.

After the Lord's Prayer, my father called each of us in turn to the middle of the circle to take the Bible and read a bit of verse that he had selected. Though he hardly read anything else, my father had that deep knowledge of the Holy Book that comes from a lifetime of study and reading. Once all the children had read, my mother said her weekly prayer. For 10 or 15 minutes, she spoke to God about her wishes for just about everyone she knew, from the smallest child to the world as a whole, hoping to be led to peace and justice, and asking protection for the family and all she loved. My father closed the service by asking God to bless the family in the coming week, and then it was time to go to church.

Like many churches with congregations richer in spirit than in money, Chapel Hill Baptist Church shared its preacher with four other churches, so he showed up only on the first Sunday of the month. Although Solomon was a deacon, he would go to church only if the preacher was going to be there. The children, however, went every Sunday to Bible Study and stayed for the service, even if there wasn't going to be any preaching.

The church lay beyond the schoolhouse, about three miles away down Church Road. We walked in most weather, but on occasion my father would drive us in the cart. Chapel Hill Baptist was a white wooden church with a bell at the top of a wide steeple. The bell rang as a call to the service, and it would also toll whenever a fallen believer was being buried in the graveyard below, an eerie sound that always spooked me. Both of these occasions were important to me as a country boy. I believed in the teachings of the church, and my spirits rose when the bell rang for the service. But I also believed just as much in spirits who haunted the earth after death. Regardless of the graveyard, I loved going to church because it meant getting away from the farm for a change of scenery to meet and play with other children.

The other building on the church grounds was an old barn used for the Homecoming festival each summer, a revival meeting that drew members home from far away. It was a week of celebrating God and preaching at a fever pitch, with potluck feasts at noon to give suste-

New Chapel Hill Baptist Church; Harrell Spruill and brother-in-law, Anthony Jordan.

nance to the faithful, and shouting and singing into the night. During Homecoming, my father would work in the mornings and come to the church in the afternoon, which meant we got off work, too. Every time I looked at that barn, I got shivers of excitement for the next revival of inspired preaching, strange new faces, good food, and the ecstasy of sinners from home and far-off lands. Even whites came out for Homecoming, and they were always welcomed because they gave good tithes. The extra tithes were necessary because lighting had to be furnished for the night services, requiring the hiring of an extra man to run the generator.

Bible Study ran from 9 until 10 with singing and praying from 10 to 11. Huddled among the wooden pews, we had a strict reading of the Bible and its lessons. Our only text was the Bible itself. The service began at eleven. My parents would come in the cart and Solomon would assume his duties as a deacon. The deacons were the most respected men in the black community. The head deacon was the only black man I knew who owned a car. Though he could not read or write very well, the head deacon was deeply religious, could count money, and ran a profitable farm. My father was much the same. Because he spent all his time working on the farm or on the road crew, and didn't waste time with idle recreation, deacon was the only social position my father possessed.

We knew it was important to him, but could not guess how much it mattered until he lost his position. I was about 13 years old when our regular minister died. The Deacon Board wanted to bring in a high-powered minister. My father had his doubts, but he was outvoted. After about two months, the high-paid minister started sending a substitute. After he did this several times, my father and two others insisted that he be fired. The rest of the board didn't agree and my father was put off the Deacon Board. After that he seemed to have lost what faith he had in people. He kept to himself even more than he had before. He was allowed back on the board when they realized they were wrong and the minister was going to keep abusing them, but the damage had been done.

Until we got older, Al and I sat with my mother in the Amen Corner, where the most fervent women worshippers held court. It was a dangerous place for a small boy. Surrounded by dozens of enthusiastic women, most of them much larger than us, we had to be alert at all times for flying elbows and flapping arms. As the service continued, the women would "get happy," standing and dancing in place, moving their arms and bodies as they shouted in heartfelt response to the calls and admonitions of the minister. As he got heated up, so did the ladies. My mother did the best she could to protect us, but at times a bump to the head could not be avoided.

The service went on for about an hour and a half. In the yard of the church we exchanged news with the neighbors, and then rode home in a slow line of carts and folks walking back to their farms and homes. The family changed clothes and ate lunch.

After lunch, Eva and Von would sit in the parlor on Sunday afternoons, singing and playing the organ, or listening to gospel records on the Victrola. It never seemed strange to me that a poor family like ours would keep a parlor with fancy furniture that was used only on rare occasions. If one person in the community had a parlor with fancy couches and an organ, the Spruills were going to have one, too. My sisters like to keep on their Sunday dresses, or go visiting to the few relatives they had permission to meet. Al and I couldn't wait to get out of our suits.

The small boys were expected to spend Sunday afternoon keeping the chickens out of the fields. The acre of stamped-down dirt and weeds was fenced in, but a determined chicken with a talent for short flights could lift itself over the fence and end up in the rows of corn or cotton. Somehow the chickens managed to stay in the yard just fine without someone watching them during the week. I only understood as I got older that my father wanted to give us something to do on Sunday afternoons when we might otherwise be making trouble with other boys.

It wasn't too hard keeping the chickens on the right side of the fence, strutting and clucking by their house. We had plenty of time to play with each other in the sun and keep one eye on the chickens, and maybe my father knew this, too. Of course, being boys, we still found the opportunity for trouble. One Sunday afternoon we stole Von's favorite doll, the one that could cry. We couldn't figure out what made it cry, but we were determined to find out. When we'd had enough of guessing, we stole it on a quiet Sunday afternoon and took it down into the woods for emergency surgery. We tried to sew it back together, but when Von squeezed the hand, it wouldn't cry anymore. Instead, it was Von who was crying over her broken toy. We felt awful—not bad enough to tell her why the doll wouldn't cry anymore, but pretty awful.

In the yard among the animals, Al and I played our favorite Sunday game, reenacting the church service from the morning. Al, a precocious and curious child, would play the part of the preacher to the hilt, shouting and stomping, modulating his voice to growl and whisper just like the man himself in the pulpit. I would be the deacon, introducing the preacher, taking up a collection, pretending to "get happy." Sometimes we would put on a mock revival like they had at Homecoming, and I would play the part of the man confessing his sins. Von and Eva would join us singing and imitating the ladies of the church.

As I chased down a chicken that fluttered and squawked near the fence, I remembered my secret Sunday mission for my mother. I peeked over at the house and determined that Solomon would be napping by now, making it safe to slip over the fence and run across the fields. Hidden by the rows of corn, I kept my bearings by heading toward the eaves of the house on the other side of our fields, my grandfather's farm. After he died, it had become enemy territory for my father.

My grandfather had sold a piece of land to each son, keeping the eight acres and farmhouse in between. When he remarried after his first wife passed away, he built his new wife Louise a new house, about a mile away from the farms. He directed that when he died he wanted his wife to move into the new house and the old family homestead should pass on to my father and his brothers and sisters.

In those days, nobody thought to make a will. We had no lawyers in the community and many could not read or write. A civil society depended on accepting each other's word as bond. When my grandfather died, however, Louise moved her children to the new house but continued to live in the old house that should have been passed on to my father and his siblings.

Despite arguments and threats, she refused to vacate the house. By the time I came along, my father didn't speak to Louise and the old farm was a forbidden zone. We weren't allowed to play with her children. My father's youngest sister caused more trouble when she married Louise's son and moved into the disputed house.

With so few houses nearby and strict restrictions on whom we could visit, it seemed cruel that the children shouldn't go over and play with our cousins. In particular, I didn't think it right that I couldn't go and read the newspaper at Louise's, which they took and we did not. My father viewed the paper as a luxury. My mission on Sundays was to go over to the enemy farm and get the comics from the paper to bring back to my mother. She would read them in secret, and then I would run them back to the house, after reading them myself, of course. Despite my father's injunction, the Spruill children often visited to play with our cousins.

After my mission was complete, the afternoon passed slowly in the yard, but Al and I didn't mind. We had each other to keep company, and if the day passed too quickly, it would soon be Monday, with chores and school and work. We happily scampered around the yard until called in to dinner.

Once every summer, the minister would come over for Sunday dinner, which turned into the biggest social event of the year for the family. Many relatives who had moved away would return for the occasion, coming home from as far away as New York City. It was a chance for members of the family to brag and show off about how well they were doing. They would show up in fancy cars and hand out pennies to the children to demonstrate to the minister how well off they were. At one memorable dinner, a relative stayed too long and a man showed up to pick up "his" expensive car. It turned out that many of them were renting vehicles to appear more prosperous than they really were.

Usually, however, we just went in for a quiet dinner and came back out to watch the chickens again until they went into their house for the night. I didn't care, though, because when the minister came there was never any food left for the children. The adults got the best part of the chicken and the kids got the feet. To my mind, I ate far too many chicken feet as a child and I still don't like them today.

Chapter 5

High School

———◆●◆———

When my oldest brother Welton and my oldest sister Carrie went off to Elizabeth City, North Carolina, to attend the teaching college there, they changed the destiny of the Spruill family. Of course, they didn't see it that way at the time, but they made it impossible for the rest of the children to stay in Travis. The black youth tended to stick around the area after high school, if they graduated at all. Those who left for Norfolk or New York City found themselves trapped in the menial jobs open to blacks with no college education. It was an exciting and rare accomplishment for Welton, and then Carrie, to leave home to train as teachers. Welton never finished, moving to Richmond before he got his degree. Carrie, however, went for two years and became the first Spruill to get a certificate in higher education. Later she went back and got her full degree. Actually, Elizabeth City State Normal College was a two-year college. So Carrie received a teaching certificate first. Then she went back to the same college after it became a four-year college. She got a B.S. Degree.

When Carrie planned one of her visits home, the children would wait outside in the yard to hear the train whistle announcing its arrival at the Travis station. "Here comes my daughter," my mother would say joyously. "Here comes my daughter!" The children would repeat, "Here comes our sister! Here comes our sister!" The corn grew between the road and our house, so we couldn't see her until she turned down the drive with her bag, waving happily, looking grown up and mature, a visitor from another world far beyond the farms and fields of Travis.

Al and I, who didn't even know what the word "college" meant, were in awe of her. We told my mother that we were going to college one day, too. Perhaps my mother knew that if one child went and showed that it was possible, the others would not see all the obstacles to higher education for blacks, but would instead see its rewards and possibilities. After Carrie got her degree, I know that I felt we had no choice but to strive to match her accomplishments.

One by one, my mother nurtured and coerced the Spruill children through high school, keeping their eyes on the prize of a college education and a better life off the farm. My father allowed us to go to school, but it was my mother's hand pushing us toward greater things. My brother Johnson went on to earn his teaching degree at Elizabeth City. William went to Union University in Richmond, Virginia, to become a minister. Unfortunately, he never finished and got married instead. Elijah never seemed to want to go to college, and joined the Navy, where he served his country for 30 years.

By the time I skipped seventh grade and moved to the upper school, I knew I would go to college. I respected the farmers and their work ethic, but I wanted a real career where effort was rewarded on an equal and consistent basis. Farmers gave all their time and energy to their land, and got back just enough to keep the family alive for another season. This determination to go to college sustained me during my struggles to get a decent education in Travis.

Luckily for me, some of our neighbors in the community shared this passion for education as a tool for raising up our people. I attended a high school that had been founded by such a man. The school system at the time did not provide an upper school for blacks, so S.P. Dean raised the money to build one. The community provided the labor, and Mr. Dean became the principal and taught mathematics.

Most folks, however, did not have an example such as my sister Carrie. Of the 32 students who began high school with me, only 8 were left by graduation day. The girls went through the dramas of teenage pregnancy in a country village; they had to drop out of school and go into hiding until they gave birth, and some were put out of the church for their sin. Many of the boys went north to Norfolk or New York City to follow others who had gone in pursuit of higher wages and good times. Without an education, however, their employment options would be limited for their entire lives. They could be porters, day laborers, or domestic servants. Of the eight graduates, I was the only one to go to college.

Tyrell County Training high school was in Columbia, about six miles from Travis down Highway 64, the main paved road in the area. The distance meant that I rode the bus instead of walking. A man named Rosenwald had given the black community buses to get their children to high school, and the drivers were students at first. My first year in high school was also the first year that the state provided transportation, and real drivers, for blacks.

I was nervous and scared about high school, a condition that continued most of the way until graduation. I was a year younger and much smaller than the other boys. My father kept us close to home, so my best friends were my siblings, and I had trouble catching up with those who had already made friends. Solomon also insisted that the boys keep wearing short pants, which came down to the knees, far past the age when long pants would have been appropriate. I spent the eighth and ninth grades in short pants, often getting into scuffles with other boys who would tease me. I suppose it was my father's way of keeping the boys under his finger, preventing them from thinking they were grown men and causing trouble. It had the effect, however, of isolating us, making us different in an environment where being

High School Graduation

*Harrell standing in front of Old Salem Baptist Church
that looks like Chapel Hill Baptist Church.*

different made it hard to make friends.

Opportunities for a social life, however, were rare.
Men's basketball was the only team sport. The only
dance we had was the senior prom. The focus for all of
us was attending class and getting home in the afternoons to help our families or work a job. The one social
activity I participated in had to do with farming. As a
member of the New Farmers of America, the black
version of the Future Farmers of America, I traveled to
Greensboro for competitions. These trips were the only
time I ever left the county.

A high school education consisted of four years of
varying levels of mathematics, science, English, and
social studies. The boys were required to take agriculture
classes covering all aspects of farming life, including
animal husbandry and blacksmithing. The girls took
home economics, learning to cook, sew, and run a
household. A student graduated at 15 years of age. As I
went through school, I realized that I was going to be
unprepared for college. The teaching was inconsistent.
Certain teachers in English and the humanities were so
poor that I felt I had only the most basic understanding of
reading and writing. The agriculture teaching was excellent, but I knew such topics would be of little use to me.
Mr. Dean had been a good math and science teacher in
the first two years, but then he started a credit union to
help black people save money and buy homes and
businesses. This difficult project took up all his time and
he gave up teaching.

By the time I graduated from high school, it was
such a common occurrence for the Spruills that my
parents didn't even attend the ceremony. They had been
to many other such ceremonies, and the graduation was
held in the afternoon on a weekday. It might seem
strange that my mother, who had pushed me so hard to
get good grades, would miss the ceremony, but I understood that when you got busy on the farm you couldn't
just leave.

In my final year of high school, I already knew that I
would do things a little differently from my siblings. I had
read much of Booker T. Washington's writings and shared
his philosophies. Instead of going to Elizabeth City
Teacher's College, I wanted to follow Washington's footsteps to the Hampton Institute in Virginia. My agriculture
teacher had spent two years there and counseled me
about the work-study program in which a student could
work for the college and pay a reduced tuition. Because I
had no money of my own, and my parents could not be
asked to help, I set myself the goal of attending Hampton
on a work-study grant.

Despite my intentions, I didn't know if I could gain
admission to Hampton or if I would be able to succeed in
my studies there. I had serious doubts about my prepara-
tion. I knew for certain, however, that I needed to save
money. In the summers, I no longer went out to pick
white potatoes or to help harvest peanuts.

Instead, I got a job at age 13 working for a white
farmer about two miles away. In the morning, I'd walk
over to his farm before sunrise and meet him at six to get
my instructions on what to accomplish that day. He rarely
helped me out with the cultivating and plowing. He was a
businessman with duties in town, and the farm was a
way to make some money off his 30 acres. I had one
hour for lunch, which he provided. The maid would
serve me in the tiny pantry off the kitchen, and when I
was finished I made myself scarce in the shade of the
barn until it was time to go back to work. I made $1.00
for a 12-hour day.

I worked for this farmer for two summers, and he
was very disappointed when I left to take a job with
another farmer who was paying $1.25 a day, though I
didn't get lunch. My new job had me managing a much
larger farm of 60 acres. The farmer treated me well, but
he was the lazy sort who told me what to do and then
walked up the road to the post office to sit on the porch
and gossip until suppertime. He was one of the few

white men I knew who did not own a car and had to go around on foot like black people.

By this time, I had put together a bicycle for myself out of spare parts that I had borrowed or begged. It took me three years to put together that bicycle and though it wasn't anything to look at, it saved me a lot of time walking to work. I stored it in the barn at my new job. I began to notice the farmer's pretty 16-year-old daughter hanging around the barn, and soon I saw her riding on my bike. At first she only went around the barn as if she was learning to ride, but after a few days she went out into the road. She never asked me if she could use it, which didn't strike me as strange. White girls did not talk to black boys. She just assumed she had every right to ride on it. It was impossible to ask her not to do so. Every time I saw her on it I was sure that bike was about to break down. I knew how rickety it was and how much make care was needed to make sure nothing fell off. Speaking directly to her, however, was too much of a risk. Although the money was good and the farmer nice, I was happy when the summer ended so I would no longer have to worry about my bicycle.

In my senior year, I worried about getting into Hampton until I met the Dean of Women at a banquet. After her speech, she encouraged me to apply as a work-study student, and gave me some tips on applying. In the spring, I was accepted into the college I so dearly wanted to attend.

During the excitement of prom and graduation, I realized that my money wasn't going to be enough even with the work-study grant. I deferred my admission for another year and went to work at a sawmill in Columbia where I earned the incredible salary of $17.50 a week. I thought I was rich even though I paid my father $5 a week for room and board. The area where I worked was known as "green alley." After a log went under the saw blade, I carried the green parts of the logs to another room to be stacked onto mule carts. I had no gloves, and the wood tore up even my tough farmer's hands. If there was no wood for the mill, we were put to work in the forest sawing pine trees into six-foot lengths with a double-handled saw, then loading them onto the back of a truck.

For more than a year I performed this hard labor at the mill and lived at home to save money. I was sustained by dreams of college and a better life away from Travis. Even though I had taken a year to make tuition, I was still only 18 when I boarded the bus to leave the state of North Carolina for the first time in my life.

Chapter 6

College Man

———————◆●◆———————

When I boarded the bus for Norfolk, headed for the back seat reserved for blacks, I had never set foot outside the borders of North Carolina. Only rarely had I ventured beyond Tyrell County to Greensboro. I knew that not only would I be younger than most of my classmates at the Hampton Institute, I had almost no experience of life. My father kept the Spruill children close the farm, in many ways isolating us from the rest of the community. I had grown up with few friends outside my siblings, and knew very little about romance and social behavior. I was still a shy farm boy, more at home in the fields than at a party, with serious doubts about my ability to make it academically in college.

Yet I took my hard-earned money and I got on the bus in the fall of 1942. Perhaps some of my courage had to do with the path my siblings had set before me, showing me that it could be done. My mother's confidence in me was also a rock, as well as the work ethic I had inherited from my father. I also shared my mother's belief of the importance of education both to me and to black people in general.

In Travis at that time, we tended to accept the unjust racial situation. That meant using the black entrance to stores in Columbia, not being able to eat in restaurants with whites or use the bathrooms in public places, sitting in the back seat of the bus or standing if a white person asked for your seat. When boarding the bus, you had to wait until all the whites got on, and then you could board if there was room for you.

Some whites were, in fact, kind, and even if they all didn't want to see black people achieve something greater in life, they didn't try to stop us from trying. Others were quite cruel, and brought to our lives the threat and reality of violence and humiliation. After I went to college, for example, the community made plans to turn my old elementary school building into a center for black events and meetings. The Ku Klux Klan burned it to the ground rather than see this happen. My old high school principal, S.P. Dean, was under constant threat after he started his credit union for blacks. A group of white people finally had enough and kidnapped him for a week. When he was finally returned, he had a nervous breakdown and was never the same. In a similar event, my agriculture teacher in high school later created an experimental farm that hired both black and white youth to learn the art of farming. A mob came by his house one day, angry about the mixing of the races on land owned by a black man. He hid under his bed while they searched the house, and I believe if they had found him they would have lynched him.

I had always accepted the situation in the South since I was old enough to realize that vast gulf between blacks and whites. Almost all the blacks I knew were of the same mind, though independent spirits like Von and Al chafed badly under the restrictions. We knew our place, and so long as we stayed in it, nothing terrible would happen to us. If we strayed, we also were certain that we would be punished, often arbitrarily and severely. As I went to college, the Civil Rights Movement was just getting started. Hampton, for example, exchanged black students with white colleges in the North, allowing white students to spend a semester at the Institute. It would be a long time, however, before the movement's leaders convinced the black populations as a whole that through struggle and activism they could dismantle the entire system of institutionalized racism. I saw a college educa-tion as the only way for black people to take a step forward without getting their heads crushed.

I was scared of all the traveling it would take to get up to Virginia, but luckily there were two people on the bus who were also going to Hampton. I just pretended like I knew what I was doing and followed them as we took buses, trolleys, and a ferry to Newport News and more buses to school. The Dean of Students warmly welcomed us and sent us off to register for classes and get our physicals. I had never before been to see a doctor because my mother used home remedies for illnesses. At Hampton, however, they had an excellent health program.

If I was worried about being lonely away from home, I found I had no reason to fear. I was assigned to a room with 12 other men. We slept in bunk beds stacked three high. Unfortunately, I was the only work-study student among my roommates, so from the start I was on a different path. They did not have to worry too much about money, except how to get a few dollars to spend on beer and dances, and they had a lot of free time to hang around talking and joking. I already suffered from low self-esteem, and the teasing of my roommates did not help. They thought I was just a poor, green country boy, and I guess I was. But I still never once wished that I was back on the farm.

I only enrolled in nine semester hours because I knew I had a poor academic foundation. My doubts were proven correct, and I struggled to make grades even in these few classes, especially English. I had to go see that professor twice a week for extra help. The teachers at Hampton were dedicated to making sure that even a mediocre student such as me found success in the end.

I also started my job in the carpentry shop. At first I simply swept up and straightened the shop after classes were over for the day. It was boring and too easy to hold my interest, but it was the job I had been assigned to earn my grant. After a month, I got a second job in the school cafeteria. The manager of the campus mill noticed how hard I worked and gave me another part-time job. I worked whenever I could because I needed to make enough money to return the next year as a regular student. It wasn't that I minded the teasing or the work—I just knew I needed to spend as much time as I could studying if I wanted to take on a full load of classes.

The only time I ever felt depressed about my jobs was the afternoons when I had to push a cart of lumber across campus, shoving it along past the halls where the men hung out on the porch or the corner, smoking and wasting time. I envied the students who could do that, and I felt bad as they watched me sweating over that cart.

In addition to jobs and classes, Hampton expected students to attend church every Sunday and a concert every Sunday night. A matron watched over the dormitory and kept us in line. Even for those who didn't have to work and study every minute, it was a staid, supervised life as a freshman. Once or twice a month, we would go into town to see a movie or go to a dance at the women's dormitory. I had some crushes on girls at those dances, but I was shy and didn't really know how to approach them. My roommates called me a wallflower.

In the break before the second semester, I took the long journey home to visit my parents. I had passed all my courses. After all my new experiences, it was strange to get back to Travis and find that everything was just the way I left it, including my father. Though I had been gone for several months, all he wanted to talk about was the things that needed to be done on the farm. He never asked me about my schooling or adventures. I spent many hours, however, talking with my mother, who couldn't seem to hear enough, though she must have heard the same kinds of stories from the siblings who had gone off before me. I had felt homesick during the first semester, but by the end of winter break I was ready to get back. I knew for certain that I wasn't missing anything in Travis.

Every month the school sent me a statement informing me how much money I had saved. Eventually, I had enough in the bank to return the following year without working. I also thought a lot about my course of study and decided to transfer out of the trade school and try for a pre-med degree. Because World War II was continuing and I knew I would eventually be drafted, I took the test for the pre-med program with the idea of coming back to school after my service, whenever it might end, and beginning again in the medical field. I had good grades and excellent teachers in chemistry, biology, and physics. I passed the test and was assured of a spot.

During the second semester, the draft began to take its toll on the men of Hampton. One by one, my crowded room of 12 men dwindled, some of them never to return from their service. As I walked around campus, it became rare to run into a male student. Finally, in April of 1943, I was selected. Hampton had a policy that students who were drafted would be given the grade they had in the class at that time. I passed all my classes and was given credit for one year of schooling. I knew it would be a long time, however, before I was able to take it up again.

Chapter 7

In the Navy

———————◆●◆———————

When I got my draft letter, I didn't feel resentful about having to leave college after so much work, nor did I feel particularly afraid of fighting. The rest of the men in school and around the country had gone before me, and I knew that many of those younger than me would also have to serve.

Thousands of young black men from all over Virginia converged at an Army base outside Newport News to take physical exams. The armed services were still strictly segregated and we were led by white officers. Once I passed the physical, a supervisor told me that I would join the Navy. The recruits had no choice in the matter, but I was pleased to go into the Navy, where Elijah was already serving. He had been at Pearl Harbor during the Japanese attack.

A skills test determined that I was to specialize in diesel mechanics, and the prospect of learning a trade while getting paid excited me. I tried not to think about where I might end up, on what battlefield, and how far away from home. I was determined to get as much benefit as I could from the Navy while they required me to serve.

I didn't struggle as much as other folks at Basic Training at the Great Lakes Naval Training Station outside Chicago. From living with my father, I was used to strict discipline, hard labor, rising at dawn, being yelled at, and even getting beat. It wasn't that far from my normal life,

Navy Photo of Harrell S. Spruill (1943).

though I noticed other men took a long time getting used to military life, and some never did.

At the end of 16 weeks of training, some sailors shipped out immediately to combat zones. I needed eight more months of training, however, to gain my rating as a diesel mechanic. Coincidentally, the Hampton Institute served as the base for much naval training. I was soon back at the old college, living in the same dorms, eating in the same dining hall. After completing training, I was assigned to the Naval Training Station in Corpus Christi, Texas, where many naval aviators were trained.

When I arrived at Corpus Christi, I was a Seaman Second Class. I knew I couldn't stay at such a low pay grade for long. I was still thinking about what might happen after the war. I needed to save money so I could go back to college whenever the chance came. One of the things I loved about the Navy was that it rewarded hard work and study with both prestige and money. This system clicked with everything my mother had told me about the value of an education, and with everything my father had taught me about the value of a day's work. In the real world, it didn't always work so perfectly, but in the Navy any kind of man could rise by his own initiative.

Harrell was a member of the Hampton Wrestling Team.

By acquiring knowledge and taking tests, I could increase my grade and my pay. I worked my way through three levels of training, until I was Fireman First Class, wearing one red stripe around my sleeve. ("Fireman" was the rating but it had nothing to do with fighting fire; the training was in mechanical engineering.) I also became a Motor Machinist Third Class, repairing diesel engines and handling the small craft that picked up pilots who had trouble with their planes. Sometimes the pilots were unharmed and sometimes they were wounded. A few times a month, however, I had to take the little launch out into the Gulf of Mexico and retrieve a dead pilot. I had always feared dead bodies, but picking up the bodies of my fellow service members helped me see that there was nothing to be afraid of.

The whole time I was in Texas I prayed that the war would end before I got involved in the combat end of it. Unfortunately, after a little more than a year, my company got orders to ship out. We were to be given special training for the invasion of the Japanese home islands, though we didn't know the location. We reached California by train and then boarded a cargo ship for the six-day journey to Hawaii. As soon as we arrived, we heard the rumors that the United States had the atomic bomb and would soon drop it on Japan. After only a few days of training, we were given light duty around the base. Our leaders seemed certain that the bomb would end the war, but I still kept praying for peace until it was a fact that the war was over.

After the Japanese surrender in August 1945, we continued on light duty, working as little as six hours a day. I wasn't used to having so much free time, and because there wasn't much to do on the island in Hawaii, I got a job cleaning up the base barbershop. Between my two sources of income, I sent home a lot of money for my mother to keep safe for me. I now dreamed of going into business with my nest egg once I got out of the service. I was no longer interested in the pre-med program because I had lost three years and wanted to get started on a career as soon as possible.

My service in the Navy ended in March 1946 when my company was declared surplus and shipped home for discharge. I was mustered out as a Motor Machinist Second Class, having picked up many skills, seen a wider part of the world, and sent a good bit of money home. My experience in the service was positive overall, helped by the fact that I was spared the suffering of actual combat. I understand that many blacks had traumatic experiences during World War II, due to their terrible treatment at the hands of white officers. Al, for example, was drafted after high school graduation and spent six long months in the Aleutian Islands, hating every minute of it. He disliked risking his life for freedom when he had none.

The worst thing that happened to me racially in the Navy occurred in Corpus Christi. One morning all the black men were called from their barracks and ordered to line up. Nobody told us the reason, but I guessed as soon as I saw a white girl coming down the line with an escort of angry white officers who looked at us like each of us was guilty of a horrible crime. She stopped at each man and looked him carefully in the face as he stood at attention. After she examined everyone, we were dismissed without explanation. I found out later that she had been raped, but the assailant turned out to be a white sailor from off the base. I hate to think what would have happened if she had wrongly fingered one of the black men from my unit.

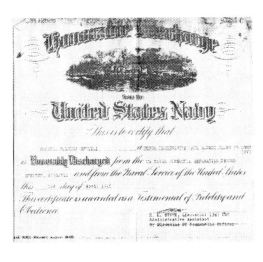

More typical of my time in the Navy was the train ride from Texas to California. As we rode through Texas and Oklahoma, the cars were divided in half by a canvas sheet that kept the black and white sailors separate. As soon as we crossed out of the Jim Crow states, the canvas was ripped down and the young men of both races mingled happily together the rest of the way. For most us, black or white, it was our first trip across the country, and the shared adventure brought us together.

Farm Activities

Photo of the barns at the Tracys Landing Farm.

Sketch of the new barn design for the Tracys Landing Farm.

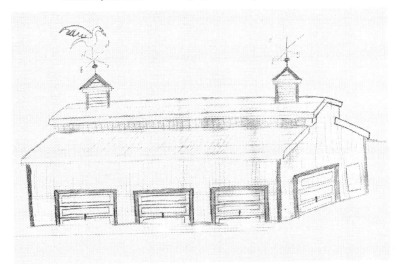

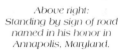

Above right:
Standing by sign of road
named in his honor in
Annapolis, Maryland.

Above left:
Spruill on his tractor;

Earl Jones, Harrell Spruill
& James Jordan;

Repairing the old barn;

James Jordan
working on the roof;

and, below,
Wallace Williams,
vounteer from First Baptist
Church and farm helper.

James Jordan built this structure for the top of the barn to hold the metal weathervane.

Fun on the Farm

Left: Children visit the farm in the summer in chaperoned groups.

Below: Visit of Maryland Forward Students to the Spruill Farm in 2002.

Following pages show people young and old enjoying a day on the farm.

Retirement

June 1983

Aris T. Allen presenting an award to Harrell Spruill.

Left to right at the Retirement Luncheon: Harrell, Pearl, Kecia and Kevin Spruill and Rev. Elihu Hamilton.

Conference Meeting

November 2005

Dr. Charlestine Fairley, Annetta Spruill, Harrell Spruill and Aris T. Allen, Jr. planning for Sojourner-Douglass College to share the farm land with the college.

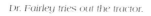

Dr. Fairley tries out the tractor.

Harrell Spruill looks forward to spending many more years on his farm enjoying life with his wife Annetta, his children, and groups of students and children who share his love of farming.

Shown left: Mr. Spruill is a faithful member of the First Baptist Church of Annapolis, Maryland.

61

Chapter 8

Back to School

———◆●◆———

Like many veterans of World War II, I returned home lamenting the lost time and hoping to catch up in a hurry. This meant I wanted to get my degree as soon as possible and get started on a career and a family. Because I had enjoyed working with engines in the Navy, I decided my best option was to pursue a three-year diploma certificate in Diesel and Auto Mechanics at Hampton.

Not only had the war kept me from my ambitions, I had not visited my family in three years. I knew my mother missed me terribly, and I wanted to believe that my father did, too. I came home in triumph, feeling confident about my future. I had done a lot of growing up in the Navy. My mother greeted me like a hero, and even my father seemed happy to see me. Some big changes had taken place. The house now had electricity and indoor plumbing.

When I asked about the money I had sent home for safekeeping, my mother didn't reply right away. I knew she was hiding some bad news from me. Finally I got her to admit that she had used most of the money to pay for college tuition for Von and Eva. Both my sisters had gone to Elizabeth City for their teaching degrees while I was away.

When my mother told me the money was gone, I felt physically sick. I went to bed for two straight days, something I had never done before and have never done since. My mother called Von, who had a job teaching in a school about an hour away. She came over to the farm and talked to me sweetly, full of gratitude for the money. She had always been like a mother to me, and as soon as I saw her, I regretted all the crying I had done. Instead of understanding why my mother had to use the money on Von, I thought only of myself. The Navy had given me the opportunity to make good money, and I knew that the GI Bill would pay all my tuition expenses. Eva and Von had no such opportunities, and my father would not help them. When Solomon took Von to the train station to go to college, he gave her 25 cents, with the advice that if she wanted to come home, she could always have grub and shelter for free. Now Von had a good job because I had paid for her training. She paid me back right away. I put the money in the credit union.

The next two weeks were the happiest I spent on the farm. I met my father in the morning for a helping of my mother's delicious cooking, then let him decide what I would do that day. Whatever the chore—chopping grass out of the cotton, pulling weeds from the corn, fixing equipment, watering animals—I enjoyed the labor, feeling like I was a help to my father, who had aged a lot since I went away. He hired workers to help at harvest time, but otherwise did the work himself. I overheard him proudly telling people how his son had come home from the war just to help him on the farm.

One evening Eva called me from Elizabeth City and asked me to pick her up the next morning. She was done for the semester and was coming back home to live. I went over there early in the morning without telling anyone and brought her home. By the time Eva was settled, my father was already out in the field. When I went to join him, he was angry at me for not having told him that I would be gone. I told him where I had been, which only seemed to make him angrier. He was always of a mind that his children should be responsible for themselves, and the farm should come ahead of everything except school. To him, I guess it was a betrayal of his authority to go pick up Eva when she could have taken the train or made other arrangements. We almost came to blows. That night, once I calmed down, I went to speak to him about our argument.

"This is my house," he told me. "If you don't want to obey me, there's the door." He wouldn't listen to anything else I tried to say. Early the next morning, I left for Swansquarter to stay with my sister Carrie. For the rest of the summer I did errands and helped her out around the house. It was too late to get a real job, so for the first time in my life I was bored, a feeling I did not appreciate. Time seemed to pass so slowly with nothing to do but think.

That summer morning in the fields was the end of my relationship with my father. Perhaps it had been dying for a long time before that. It had never been great, but I still missed it terribly after it was gone. I never understood him as a man, and he never seemed to understand anyone else in the family. Only my brother Johnson, the diplomat, could get him talking and relaxed. It had taken so much for him to

Harrell S. Spruill was a member of Hampton Institute's Wrestling Team in 1947.

carve out "Solomon's Castle" off the Back Road in Travis that he became a despot of his little domain. Though he would never show it, he must have been afraid of the crops failing, his family starving, losing the land. Thus he had to control everything, and he seemed to view even his family as obstacles to his control. Seeing what that kind of life had cost him, I was more determined than ever to find a trade that allowed me to work hard and gain a comfortable living.

For my mother's sake, I still visited home. Nothing, however, changed with Solomon. Each time he was cold and would hardly speak to me, as if I was not his son. My mother was always the same, waiting out by the porch when she knew I was coming, looking down the road for my car, hugging me so tight I could hardly breathe.

The one thing that did change in those years after the war was me. It was as if all that traveling and learning in the Navy had washed away the low self-esteem and shyness from Travis. I was no longer on the work-study program at Hampton, so I was free to pursue social activities just like a normal student. I joined the wrestling

Harrell Spruill (front row, second from left) was a member of the Omicron Social Club at Hampton Institute.

Hampton Institute's Wrestling Team in 1947.
Harrell S. Spruill is on the far right of the photo in the front row.

club and pledged the Omicron Social Club. The pledging period lasted for two months and we had to put up with a bunch of stuff before we became brothers. I wanted to be in the club so badly that I put aside my shyness and really impressed them. When I came home, my mother and father didn't really understand what it meant to me to have made it into the club, but Von knew and was so proud of me. When she told me fondly how I had changed for the better, I thought with shame of how I had cried and cursed her when I heard she had used my money for college. Eventually Von helped me put my guilt out of my mind because she was such a forgiving, understanding sister.

My happy college life swept time forward. I won two CIAA wrestling championships in the 145-150 pound class, a feat I owed partly to all those dusty matches in the farmyard with Al. I traveled all over the country to live with friends on breaks, and worked in an auto shop in Newport News. I did well in all my classes because I was truly interested in and talented at fixing engines.

I decided to spend Christmas of 1948, my senior year in the program, at home. I could put up with my father for a few days if it meant seeing my mother. He was as cold as ever and we spent the time staying out of each other's way in the small house. It was the last time I saw him alive.

My father Solomon passed away in the spring of 1949, right before I earned my certificate in Diesel and Auto Mechanics. My mother noticed the mule standing at the gate one morning and when she went to the field she found her husband lying by the plow, dead of a stroke. He was 62 years old.

All the Spruill children returned to Travis for the funeral. Al was at Cornell University and would soon go to Iowa State for his master's degree. Von was studying for her master's degree at Penn State. They both studied in the North because they were not permitted to attend Southern graduate schools. The state government paid them to go out of state, and they actually made more money going to school than they could teaching.

Many good things were said about my father at the funeral, and I still believe there was much good to say. His work ethic was a credit to any man. He was religious and had loved the church and served it well. He had earned the respect of the community, including powerful white people, a difficult and rare accomplishment. I wish I could say there had been reconciliation before his death. As time has passed, my respect for his sacrifices for the family has grown. I think I understand and love him more now than I did when he was alive.

None of the children had been very close to him. My mother, however, had loved him deeply and with a great understanding of his nature and ways. Over the years after his death, men would come courting, but she wouldn't hear them at all. She preferred to stay alone with her Bible and her memories.

HAMPTON INSTITUTE

HAMPTON, VIRGINIA

THIS IS TO CERTIFY THAT

Harrell Solomon Spruill

IS A GRADUATE OF THE REGULAR THREE-YEAR COURSE IN

AUTOMOBILE AND DIESEL MECHANICS

AND WAS GRANTED THE DIPLOMA OF THE INSTITUTE

MAY 30, 1949

_____   _____
DEAN OF FACULTY   PRESIDENT

*Harrell Spruill completes the necessary coursework to graduate
from the Automobile and Diesel Mechanics Program at Hampton Institute in 1949.*

Although my mother had her Bible, the Spruill children all felt it would be best if someone stayed with her and kept the farm running. My father had hidden $5,000 in cash in the barn, so my mother had more than enough money. William, who had settled in Richmond after a brief time at Union University, decided to stay in Travis and work the farm. My brother and sisters, already established in their careers, would pay him $25 a month each. Because I was a poor student and couldn't contribute anything, I kept my reservations about the arrangement to myself. William had a family in Richmond to support, and he wouldn't find any social life to speak of in Travis. I put it out of my mind so I could return to school and proceed in finishing my classes.

In the spring of 1949, seven years after I first left home for Hampton, I graduated with a certificate and diploma in Diesel and Auto Mechanics. I had made two close friends with the same interests. We all spent the next six months in Chicago going to school for body and fender training. We worked during the day and attended class at night, living in the same rented room, cooking meals for each other. My buddies liked to go out on Saturday night, but they understood that I preferred to stay home. One night they came knocking desperately on the basement window, begging me to let them in. They had been too forward with a gang member at a bar, and he had chased them all the way home. They never did go out on Saturday again as long as we were in Chicago.

By the time we came back to Virginia, we had a good amount of experience and knowledge in auto work among the three of us. We had sat up many nights dreaming about opening our own shop and going into business for ourselves. We decided to pursue our dream in Portsmouth, Virginia. While my friends hunted for a space to rent for the shop, I went to Travis to make sure my mother was doing all right.

Hampton Institute

Hampton, Virginia

This is to Certify that

Harrell Solomon Spruill

has completed the three-year curriculum in the Trade Division and, having maintained a satisfactory standard of excellence in character and scholarship, is entitled to this

Diploma

In Testimony Whereof, we have affixed our names and the seal of the Institute.　　　　May 30th, A.D. 1949

Chairman, Board of Trustees

Dean of Faculty

President

I found her in good physical health, but I could sense she was worried. I found out why as soon as I started walking around the farm. The yard, usually so full of animals, was bare and quiet. I walked through the fields to the forest and found that many of the trees that my father would never sell for lumber had been harvested. When I asked William about these changes, he said he had sold the livestock and trees because he was leaving to go back to Richmond and needed money for his family. He had not even told my mother that he was departing the next day. When my mother overheard us arguing, she got sick and went to bed.

I took a walk around the farm and tried to decide what to do about my mother. The land was in bad shape and I knew my father would not be happy that his castle has been left to fall into disrepair while his beloved wife was left to fend for herself. It was one of those cold

Harrell S. Spruill receiving a B.S. degree from the President of Hampton Institute.

December days when the forest drips, the sky looks dreary, and it seems like spring will never come. I thought about the excitement of starting a new business in a new town with my friends, and how hard I had worked to get to a point where I could really start my life.

In the end, however, I loved my mother too much to leave her behind alone. Instead of a new adventure in Portsmouth, I returned to Travis. I stayed there from December 1949 until September 1950, when I returned to Hampton to get a degree in Industrial Education.

After I made my decision to stay, I went into my mother's room where she lay with eyes closed under the quilt, sick with worry. When I told her that I would stay until at least the new school year, she was excited that one of her boys was going to take care of the farm. I kept reminding her that I would only be there temporarily, which she understood. After I dropped my brother at the bus station, I went home and started on the chores.

There wasn't all that much to do on a small farm in the winter so I had plenty of time to apply to Hampton's teaching program. My father had taught me well and I knew exactly what to do to get ready for spring planting. My mother and I continued the family prayer on Sunday morning, and I took her to church to hear the preaching.

GENERAL MOTORS INSTITUTE

This is to Certify That

HARRELL S. SPRUILL

Has Completed the Requirements of the Four-Week Course in the

AUTO MECHANICS TEACHER TRAINING PROGRAM

and in recognition thereof is awarded this

CERTIFICATE

Given under our hands and seal at Flint, Michigan,

this **22nd** day of **July, 1955.**

Department Chairman

President, General Motors Institute

Though I missed my friends and regretted that I wasn't in business, I knew I had made the right decision. I farmed through the summer, enjoying the outdoors, but looking forward to school.

I arranged for pickers from the community to come in during the harvest season when I would be off at school. My cousin would rent the farm when I left, using our equipment and mules. My mother would get the proceeds from half the crop. Von taught school nearby so she could check on our mother and keep an eye on my cousin, and could come home from time to time. In this way, we would keep the farm running.

Hampton Institute

The Trustees of Hampton Institute upon the recommendation of the Faculty have conferred upon

Harrell Solomon Spruill

the degree of

Bachelor of Science

with all the rights, privileges and honors pertaining thereto. Given under the seal of the Institute at Hampton, Virginia on the second day of June nineteen hundred and fifty-two.

The teaching degree was a two-year program and was much more difficult than my previous certificate. I struggled along, earning grades just good enough to pass. I surprised myself, however, by excelling in my student teaching. I didn't have the head for pure academics, but I was good at teaching others to acquire the concrete skills I already had in auto repair. Teaching had not been my first choice, but I grew to love doing it.

Von was the only one who came to my graduation. She drove my mother north to Eva's house, but she was in poor health and could go no further, though I knew she wanted to come. Having Von in the family was like having two mothers.

Hampton had an excellent placement center and I quickly got two good offers. I decided to take a job at Alcorn A&M College in Mississippi. The job involved starting an auto mechanics and body and fender program from scratch. I bought a car with my savings, the first I ever owned, and on my way south I stopped to see my mother. She was feeling better and living with a girl who Von hired to take care of her. I was the last of her children to find his path in life. She was proud that she could finally tell her friends that all of her children had found their vocations.

Chapter 9

A New Career

Alcorn A&M wanted me to report in July, a few months before school began. Eager to start my career, I drove down in two days and checked into the men's faculty dormitory. I soon found out why they needed me so early. In addition to starting up the industrial program, I would be responsible for servicing all the farm equipment, the buildings and grounds equipment, and the school bus used to take the teams to games.

Before I had time to recover from the shock of hearing my additional responsibilities, they brought in a test for me to prove that I could do my job. The school had an old cement mixer made in the early 1900s that had been donated by another university as surplus property. It hadn't run in years, but they wanted me to fix it. Recognizing that I was being watched carefully, I spent two weeks getting that ancient hulk into showroom condition. Every spare minute when I wasn't repairing tractors and lawn mower I worked on that cement mixer. I even painted it. The carpentry and brick-laying people were thrilled and amazed that they could use the mixer again.

In September, I was assigned 13 students for my classes. The program would be a minor as part of a degree in Industrial Education. For some reason the president of the college didn't think I'd be doing enough to earn my salary, so he made me teach a freshman math course. He didn't realize, I suppose, that the students enrolled in my program knew nothing yet about

74

Students at South River Vocational Technical Center in Edgewater are getting a special opportunity to show off their talents this week, National Vocational Education Week. An open house will be held from 6:30 to 8:30 p.m. Wednesday in the newly built school at 211 Central Avenue East, Edgewater. Above, Susan Walton of Lothian and Lloyd Woodall of Harwood practice their cosmetology skills while Randolph Manns of Severna Park applies tape to a VW before painting it. The 374 students at the center are from Severna Park, Annapolis and south county.

mechanics and I could not expect any help from them in maintaining all that equipment. It would be several years before I trained them enough to help me with the overwhelming amount of maintenance work.

With no choice in the matter, I simply studied the math book, keeping about a week ahead of what I taught in class. The students and I learned together, but I had a feeling that it was harder for me than them. My greatest goal was not to cripple them with poor teaching as I had been in high school. Between all my tasks, I once again had no time for social activities. I spent many evenings riding on the team bus to far-away colleges for games, fixing the bus when it broke down along the way. By that point in my life, however, I recognized that there are times where you must simply keep working in the dark with your head down until you get a little daylight. The daylight always comes.

The following school year, for example, I was relieved of my math duties and had trained a few students

to help me with maintaining the school vehicles. I also had time to meet a young chemistry teacher named Claudine. She had been a medical student at Howard University and was respected among the students and faculty as a top-notch teacher. We began dating and soon fell in love. Though she left A&M for Miles College in Alabama, we continued to have a close relationship.

It was thoughts of getting married and having a family with Claudine that made me worry about my tenure at Alcorn A&M. The president could give an employee 30 days notice at any time. He would often fire a man who had just gotten married because he thought that bachelors made better employees. I knew I didn't want to be a bachelor much longer, so I started looking around for a more stable position.

With the help of the Hampton placement center, I found a job in the spring of 1954 in Annapolis, Maryland, at Wiley H. Bates High School, the black upper school for the city. The President of Alcorn offered to raise my salary and begged me to stay. My mind was made up, however. Although the pay would be less, there was a greater chance of tenure and I knew I wouldn't be fired if I got married. In September, I left Mississippi for Annapolis.

I was not sad to leave Alcorn or Mississippi. Much was going in the Civil Rights Movement. My brother Al had settled in at North Carolina A&T as a teacher and was very serious about the push for integration and equal rights. We would have many long discussions about how to correct the racial injustice in America. I was on the side of diplomacy and education, while he favored more radical action, though always peaceful. We both greatly admired the marchers and protesters who suffered so much violence attempting to gain basic rights for black people. We also both agreed that our vocation of teaching was vital for a better future for both blacks and America as a whole.

In Annapolis, I rented a room from a lady who owned a house on Lafayette Avenue. The room came under her strict code of conduct, which she dictated to me before she even showed me my new abode. The tiny room had no automatic hot water heater. She had to bring up the hot water in the morning for me to wash. I thought I would soon get a better place, but it turned out that there were few rooms available for single black males. Conditions among the races in Maryland were better than in the deeper South, if only slightly. There were still "Whites Only" signs and separate entrances. Black folks had to go out of town to visit the hospital, and blacks couldn't try on hats in the stores.

I reported to Mr. Douglas King, the principal of Bates High School, in October of 1954. When he took me down to see the shop, my heart sank. I walked around pushing over the rickety and broken chairs and stools. The tool room contained only a few tools, most of them broken or outdated. I turned on the air compressor, which made a lot of noise, telling me it hadn't been serviced in some time. The students filed in and regarded me with curiosity. They had been without a teacher for a month. Only half of them could sit because of all the broken chairs.

As they waited expectantly for their new teacher to speak, I really thought about walking out and never coming back. Mr. King had promised that the shop had good equipment and that I would find all the tools I needed to carry on the program. Though he had lied to me, these kids did not have to pay. Instead of getting angry, I put on a happy face and assured them I would teach them something worth learning. The kids in my classes were called "problem students" said to be unable to adapt in a normal classroom situation. They acted out and could be a handful, but I knew they just wanted to learn something that would help them make a living and buy the things they wanted. I found out that they had been kept busy washing and polishing cars, so, of course, they were bored.

The Anne Arundel County Board of Education was reluctant to spend any money on vocational education. They didn't like it that it was more expensive to stock a shop than an English or mathematics class. The turnover of shop teachers was high because the worst academic students were pushed into shop. The Board seemed to think that every student was going to master academic subjects and go on to college. I knew these kids in my class had a different aptitude, a talent for working with their hands and solving mechanical problems. If they weren't going on to college, how were we going to teach them skills that would make them productive members of society? We didn't have enough tools at Bates to do any real work, so we had to keep polishing and washing cars for the next two years. I did give them lectures on auto mechanics and spray painting, and sometimes we would do demonstrations in the shop. The kids were a rowdy bunch, but you could hear a pin drop when I lectured. They were enthusiastic when we actually got our hands on a project, and they learned quickly. It was those kids that kept me at Bates.

A few weeks after I got to Annapolis and ensured that my position was secure, if not attractive, I went down to Dermott, Arkansas, to marry Claudine. We were wed in a lavish church ceremony that started us off with a mountain of debt. Though I protested, she assured me that her father, a doctor, would take care of the bills. We could not afford much of a honeymoon and her parents didn't offer us one, so we spent a few days in Florida, spending money like we were rich.

Claudine had to work for her living because I made just $375 a month, so she stayed at Miles College. I hated to invite her to visit my tiny room in Annapolis because she was used to much better. The money from her parents never did materialize. After two years, I was able to rent an apartment on Spa Road and move Claudine north. She came at Christmas of 1956 and stayed two months. She did some substitute teaching in local high schools, but she

Anne Arundel Report

Thurs., Mar. 12, 1981   33

Photo by Bob Gilbert

Show of skills

Laurie Dallas, a junior at the South River Vocational Technical classes air dries the paint job she has done on a car door. Students in all areas of study, from carpentry, to engine repair to cosmetology, will demonstrate their skills at an open house from 7-9 p.m. March 18 at the school on Central Avenue in Edgewater.

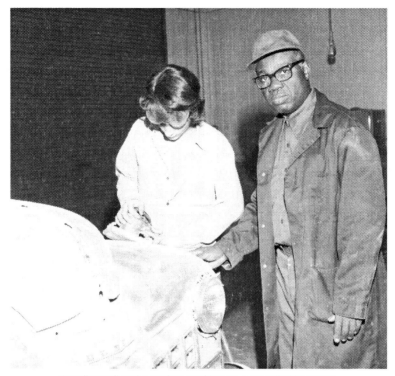

Harrell Spruill and a student working on a car painting project.

didn't get along with the students. Claudine didn't seem to like Annapolis very much. Finally she found another college position in Texas, and when that ran dry, she ended up teaching chemistry at Alabama A&M. We were separated most of the time, which made it feel like I didn't have a wife, except for the bills. Her views on life, money, and achievement were just different from mine. During the summer, she came to Annapolis and worked at Carr's Beach (a major stop on the "Chitlin Circuit"), but in the fall she would be gone again.

Without a wife around, it was easy to throw myself into the job. I started right away taking in auto work from the community and saving the proceeds for the shop at school. I bought engine blocks cheaply from the junkyard as well as many complete engines. I made stands for the engines with the electrical welder. I knew if I wanted any equipment I was going to have to scavenge, buy, or make it myself.

It took two years to get the shop into the kind of shape where we could actually do hands-on learning. The kids were so anxious to learn a trade that enrollment increased every year, even when we weren't doing much besides washing cars. By the third year, I had 50 students, and the Board of Education began to pay attention. They bought some more modern tools and equipment for the program. I could start taking in little jobs from the community that gave the kids experience and built our reputation for solid work. The small fees that we charged went right back into the shop. By 1960, I had built one of the best auto mechanics programs in Anne Arundel County. We offered electrical welding, gas welding, and auto mechanics. In addition, the Bates shop was the only one offering instruction in auto body and spray painting. We had to create a waiting list for students who wanted to get into courses.

Chapter 10

Landowner

———————◆●◆———————

My first good friend in Annapolis was a man I met when he hired me to paint his car. John Prann was a successful black businessman who understood the value of money, owned several tracts of land and a nice house, and was ambitious about acquiring property. John had come to Bates High School to teach brick laying and cement finishing, and his shop was down the hall from mine. We became friends and he began giving me advice about building for my future. He encouraged me to focus on getting a house and some land.

In 1956, John let me know that a gentleman in Washington, D.C., was searching for a buyer for land he owned in Anne Arundel County. After school we drove up to visit Mr. Turner, who ran a taxi service during the day and wanted to meet at night. I wanted to buy three acres, but he offered to sell me either 15 or 55 acres. I didn't have the money for even three acres, but as we talked late into the night he kept insisting that he would only sell 15 or 55. John thought that 15 acres would be a great investment. The property was dense woods located where Route 665 left Route 2 and joined Route 50. By the time we left Mr. Turner, I had somehow agreed to purchase 15 acres for $15,000, including a $3,000 down payment. I had only $300 cash money and my salary was just $3,000 a year, or $300 a month. John assured me I could make the payments and agreed to lend me the cash for the down payment.

After about two days, Mr. Turner called and said he

Left to right: John Prann, Harrell Spruill and Mr. Albert Baxter in 1983.

would only sell 55 acres. I drove out to his house at
about one o'clock in the morning to force him to make a
deal with me. I carried my $300 in cash in $1 bills. As we
negotiated, I kept pulling out those bills one by one and
laying them down in front of him. I could tell that the sight
of those bills stacking up was getting him excited. He
kept picking them up, rifling through them, putting them
back down. When I finally had all the money laid out, he
gave up and agreed to sell the 15 acres if I could come
up with the $3,000 down payment. I wrote a contract on
an envelope and had him sign it. I knew he was going to
change his mind, and in about two days he called me to
say he wanted to give me back my $300 and sell the 55
acres to someone else. I informed him that I had his
signature on a legal contract and I would take him to
court if I had to.

He thought about it for a day or so, probably con-
sulted with his lawyer, then agreed to sell me the land as
we agreed. I would pay Mr. Turner $100 a month for 10

years, and $60 a month plus interest to John for the cash loan. Between these obligations and other bills, I had almost nothing left of my paycheck. I was now a land-owner, however, like my father and grandfather before me, and I knew it was the right thing to struggle for.

Over the years it took to pay off Mr. Turner, I lived in a succession of boarding house rooms and cheap apart-ments. I did my own cooking, which allowed me to use the cheapest brand of food. I cut almost all social events out of my life, including dances and movies. Every spare dime I had went toward paying off the land.

By 1962, my marriage to Claudine was at its end. For most of it, we saw each other just one week at Christmas and a month during the summer. After a brief, bitter court case, the divorce was final. We were mad at each other for a while, but soon we ended as friends. We just weren't meant to be together.

Despite this protracted failure, I still wanted to be a married man. I had learned from Claudine that I needed a wife who would support our partnership and share my goals. I was looking for someone who had experiences similar to my own as I grew up in Travis, someone who knew the value of sacrifice and hard work to get some-thing better in the future. I had learned the hard way that a marriage not only is about love, but also must be a partnership for building a joined life.

I didn't know it, but I had already met the woman who would prove to be that ideal mate. In 1958, Pearl Douglas was among the many new teachers hired at Bates. I admired her long black hair and thought her to be about the prettiest

Pearl Douglas Spruill

84

woman I'd ever seen. She was 24 and I was 36 and still married, so I didn't do much aside from admire her from afar. One day, however, she came to me for advice about a car she had just bought. I helped her and we soon became fast friends.

After my divorce, we began dating. She lived in Washington, D.C., but that did not deter me. Because we had been friends for a while, I felt like we already knew each other very well. I was anxious to move on with my life and make up for lost time, so I pursued her intensely. After a whirlwind courtship, she agreed to marry me on my birthday in August 1962.

Pearl moved into the apartment I was renting and we drove to school together. We learned a lot about each other in that busy time. She was going to school in the evening for her master's degree in counseling, and I was taking classes at night to get more credits to satisfy my teaching degree. In 1963, Pearl gave birth to our first child, Kevin.

With a family to think about now, I decided to take out a mortgage on my land and build a home for us on the property. I had paid off my loan to John Prann, aided by the sale of some wood from the land and a payment from Maryland for taking about an acre for an expansion of Route 2. In 1964, we moved into our new house and I finally had the little family that I had been hoping for. Pearl continued to work and always insisted on contributing to the bills.

By this time, my mother was confined to Von's house in North Carolina, and the farm was still being run by my cousin. Soon after I moved into my new house, my mother died without ever getting to come to visit. I know she was proud of me, as she was of all her children who had come so far in life from that farm in Travis. At the time of her death, Welton was still working for Southern Rail Systems. Carrie had retired after 44 years of teaching. Johnson was principal of an elementary school in Greensville, North Carolina. Elijah had retired from the Navy and had a job at the naval base in Norfolk. Von was teaching in Plymouth, North Carolina. Von, Eva, and Al were still teaching at their schools. We all gathered for Mother's funeral and to say goodbye to this source of so much inspiration for the rest of my life. I tried to keep the things she had taught me alive in my own mind, and in the minds of my children. My approach to being a father to my son Kevin and daughter Kecia was greatly influenced by my mother.

Integration finally came to Anne Arundel County in 1966. Bates High School, which had served as the center for black education in Annapolis for so many years, was to be assigned white teachers and some black teachers would go to schools that had been previously all white. All the teachers were brought into the library and told our new assignments. Pearl was sent to Southern Senior High School, a place to which she was afraid to go because there had been many problems in that area between the races. It turned out that she was happy there and the officials at the school went out of their way to make things comfortable for the new teachers.

Because Bates was the only school that taught body and fender, the white students would be bused over to it and I would stay on. The shop expanded for the white children, and we got funds for new paint guns and other equipment.

Despite my experiences in the South, I had no problems teaching white students. I knew it was my duty as a teacher to judge the students on their performance in class, not their skin color. Some of my black students struggled and wanted special treatment, but I treated everyone the same. I told them at the start of integration that even if they didn't learn anything about auto mechanics in the class, I would be pleased if they learned to get along with each other. Even if they didn't take up the trade as a career, the basic philosophy of mutual understanding and respect would serve them well in any area of life.

Chapter 11

Back on the Farm

———◆●◆———

The old saying goes that you can take the man off the farm, but you can't take the farm out of the man. Soon after Pearl and I got settled in the new house, I began clearing and burning the brush from two acres of land to plant a big garden. Not only would growing vegetables cut down on grocery bills, it also would provide a place of work and learning for my two children. I had not wanted to stay on the farm, but I still respected its lessons. I didn't beat them like my father had beat me and I was better at talking to them than my father had been. I wanted to pass on his amazing work ethic and sense of responsibility. With house and garden, Pearl named the property "Solomon's Dominion."

Two acres of garden, however, produced many more vegetables than our family could consume. For a while, we tried giving them away to the poor, but this didn't work. They wanted us to shell the peas when we provided them, and they couldn't store food very well. We didn't feel like we were really helping. We knew we wanted our surplus to help others in the community, so we turned to helping black fraternities and sororities who needed money for building meeting places, thus establishing ownership in the minority community. We thought we would sell the extra produce and give the proceeds to the inter-Greek organization.

Our first attempt at placing a stand in front of our property off Route 2 was unsuccessful. Pearl next loaded produce in her car and sold it door-to-door throughout the community. All the vegetables that she couldn't sell immediately she froze, and we later sold them as frozen food. I enjoyed raising the garden with my children, and Pearl enjoyed going out meeting people.

We set a goal of raising $1,500 for the Greek charity in the first season. When we had $500, we gave it to the organization, earmarked for the building fund. Soon we found that the money had been given to their president to travel to Chicago for a meeting. We were upset because we saw the building fund as essential for spreading ownership in a community that owned almost nothing on its own. We never gave them any more money and instead decided to save for a scholarship for students.

I was also going to meetings to promote vocational education in the county. I met with community and trade groups, pitching the idea of a center for vocational education where we could consolidate all the different industrial programs. The programs varied widely in quality and attendance from school to school. Bates had excellent programs with waiting lists. Other schools had only minimal offerings and those students who wanted something better were out of luck. I was among many in the county who believed that a central location would be more cost-efficient and could better teach those who wanted to learn trades. Because it was a new idea requiring a large upfront investment in a new building to stock with new equipment, it took a long time to get the right people behind it. I knew it had to work eventually, however, because it made so much sense for the students and the taxpayers.

In 1976, the shop was moved from Bates to the Old Shaw Welding Shop on Chinquapin Round Road in Annapolis. Bates was closed because the school building contained asbestos. It wouldn't be long until the new vocational center was built. In 1979, the Center of Applied Technology South was completed, the realization of about 10 years of dreaming, planning, and hard work. I enjoyed going to work there every day. When parents came during Open House, they always told me how much their sons and daughters valued my classes and the center. The most rewarding part of my job was when former students opened shops of their own, able to make a living from what I taught them. Many students returned to talk with me or wrote me letters to tell me how much my guidance had meant to them. They understood that I had kept them out of trouble, believed in them when others did not, and taught them to make a living for themselves.

I served in the Anne Arundel County school system for 29 years before my retirement in 1983. I requested that one of my former students fill my position. Mr. Michael Hensen had been my aide for many years and was the perfect choice to continue the program. The school planted trees in my honor, and Albert, Von, and Eva attended the ceremony. Dr. Albert Spruill gave the keynote address and wrote about my career in his weekly newspaper column in *The Carolina Peacemaker.* Albert wrote that "those who criticize the impact of public education on the lives of young people have simply never met my brother Harrell, for he epitomizes the person who can take youngsters who lives have little meaning and turn them into skillful tradesmen." I

Tree planting in honor of Mr. Spruill for his donations to the Vica Club.

cannot think of any better legacy than leaving behind the means to provide training to youngsters to enable them to join society as productive members. Growing up in the minority underclass with much of America's potential kept beyond my reach, I have always been sensitive to this need. Only a few men live so that they change the lives of thousands or millions for the better. Most of us, however, can change the lives of the tens or hundreds that are within our reach, using whatever skills we have been blessed with.

Though teaching is a worthwhile career, very few people become rich from it. For all those years of teaching, I supplemented my income with work after school and on weekends. I was about five years ahead on paying my mortgage and my family still worked the garden and sold the extra vegetables for charity. In my retirement, I was interested in expanding our charitable work.

My plan for the far future was to get the mortgage cleared away and leave the property to my children. Kecia graduated from the University of Maryland Baltimore County (UMBC) and was working for Anne Arundel County as a social worker. Kevin ended up with a degree from UMBC and worked for the Federal Aviation Administration in Washington, D.C. I had been hearing disturbing rumors for some time that my house would be taken by the state for the building of a road. I wanted to dismiss them, but in 1985 I received an official notice that the road was planned for my property.

I knew I would need an attorney to deal with the government. I went to see one lawyer, but he steered me toward a man who had just graduated from law school and would be much cheaper. His name was Mike Roblyer and he became my trusted advisor. In fact, his services were cheaper and his advice was better. The state originally offered a low price for five acres of land, including the land my house sat on. I didn't mind giving up the property for the good of society, but I wanted to be paid a fair price for it. After many meetings, Mike got the government to pay twice as much as their original offer and in 1987 my house was torn down for the road.

We decided to build a new house on the remaining property. Pearl worked with an architect, designing the home to her specifications. She wanted space to entertain and a little bit of luxury around her. She certainly deserved it. When we moved into the new place in 1988, it became the center for social activities, meetings, and Spruill family reunions. We held these reunions once every summer and all my brothers and sisters came. I talked to Von and Albert on the phone almost every week, but the reunion was the only time I saw most of the other siblings.

For the first time in life, I had some real cash money. I had always heard that people who have been poor all their lives and suddenly get rich tend to waste their money on useless things. I told myself that I would not make that same mistake. The minority community in Annapolis had given so much to me since I had arrived, and there were those in it who needed my help now. Pearl and I had always been of the same mind about almost everything. She agreed that we should use much of the money to help others. To start, in 1987, the Spruill siblings also set up a scholarship at Chapel Hill Baptist Church in North Carolina in honor of our parents. The Solomon J. and Georgiana Wynn Spruill Scholarship helps needy black children with funds for college education.

We then decided to purchase 80 acres in Tracy's Landing in southern Anne Arundel County. I wanted to spend my retirement running garden projects on the farm for inner city kids from about

6 to 12 years old. The students would help me raise vegetables and then sell them at local stands. The profits would go to scholarships. In this way, the children would learn the work ethic of farming as well as the ins and outs of running a small business.

I had worked with the Boys and Girls Club of Annapolis in the past. Pearl served as secretary on the Board of Directors. I had given the group a van and painted it with their name and donated televisions for their clubhouse. I thought this group would make a good partner on the farm.

The first year went well, even though we had no modern equipment or machinery. I got a farmer to plant some corn so we could harvest it. Some of these children had never seen a corn plant before and everyone was excited about the possibilities of the program. I really enjoyed watching the children on the farm and seeing them sell their produce, interacting with customers. As time passed, however, kids stopped showing up for the harvesting and selling. The organization wanted to use the farm as a recreation area, bringing 150

Spruill walking through the fields on his Tracy's Landing farm.

kids at a time on buses.

One season I planted a corn crop all by myself. None of the children turned out to help. At harvest time, a television

Robert Brooks, a farm helper.

crew came to film the children harvesting the corn, as if they had helped all summer long and really learned something about farming. Out of the 1,000 children in the organization, only two or three helped me on the farm. After four years of trying to get more effort into the program, I got out. Pearl, however, stayed on as secretary until her death.

Though the Boys and Girls Club had disappointed me, I wasn't ready to give up. I leased two acres of land to the Alpha Phi Alpha fraternity. Volunteers from the fraternity would sell their crop at the farmer's market and use the profits for scholarships. Unfortunately, after about three years, the organization lost interest in the program.

I couldn't understand why the program faltered after a few years. Everyone said it was a good project for the kids but the enthusiasm would not last long. We had given away a lot of money over the years, putting in many, many hours in the fields, but I

Former student, Earl Jones, on tractor with Harrell Spruill.

93

still felt we could be doing more with the farm. Finally I joined with the First Baptist Church in Annapolis. Volunteers from the church grew the crops with me and we set up three vegetable stands. The money went for the youth in the church.

When I first bought the farm, I was lucky enough to recruit a man who could work it with dedication and honesty. Earl Jones had been my student in the 1960s. We all called him "Mr. Perfect" because he did everything just the right way and wouldn't put up with cutting corners. I recommended that he go to a special advanced school for body and fender, but he told me he wanted to be a farmer. My advice was that the small farmer was an extinct species and he was better off learning a trade. Years after his graduation, I ran into him at a car dealership. He had learned the hard way that what I said about farming was true. The foreman of the shop said that Earl was the man for any complicated work that needed to be done. He could always be counted on to be perfect. When I needed someone to come and work on a panel at school, I would always get Earl and he would never turn me down. When I bought my farm, I immediately asked him to farm for me four hours a day. He has been with me since 1993 and I could not ask for a more dependable, honest, and knowledgeable farmer. The programs we set up at the farm could never have taken place without him.

My wife Pearl passed away in 1995 at the age of 61. After her death, I was very lonely. Pearl and I had been married for 33 years. Like all long-term relationships, we had our share of problems and arguments, rough spots as we both changed in life. But we also agreed on many business and economic ventures. We had many plans for spending the future together now that all our work had paid off. I felt a huge void in my life as I looked to the future.

After I recovered somewhat from Pearl's passing, I began to notice a lady in the choir at First Baptist.

Annetta Spruill

Annetta Turner had been a member for years but I had never noticed her pleasant, sunny, caring personality. After a while getting to know her, I began courting Annetta. It turned out that she was from Elizabeth City, 60 miles from Travis and the spot where so many of my siblings got their teaching degrees. When I asked her to come over to my home, she showed up with her best friend as a chaperone because she didn't believe it proper for a lady to visit a gentleman unaccompanied. She still had those old-fashioned values that I so admired, and I knew I was pursuing a lady of quality! We were married in 1997.

Aside from the proximity of our upbringing, Annetta shares my passion for education, which was instilled in her by her mother, the same as my mother had, just like mine. She earned a bachelor's degree in education from Elizabeth City State University and moved to Maryland to teach at Huntingtown Elementary School. Before I met her, she had a son, Jay, with her first husband, and earned a graduate degree in guidance counseling at Bowie State University. She has kept as busy in retirement as when she was working, volunteering with many civic organizations. I especially admire her work as a missionary for First Baptist Church, visiting the sick and shut-ins. One of her favorite sayings is "Let your light so shine!" I'm so happy that Annetta came along after Pearl passed to let her light shine on me.

As I grew older, I began to think about moving back to the country, southern end of Anne Arundel County near the farm in Tracy's Landing, Maryland, closer to my farm in Tracy's Landing. I had bought a piece of land about one mile from my farm with a house already on it. My property in Annapolis had once been a rural parcel, but over the years the roads and shopping centers had closed in around it as Annapolis grew, and now many major roads ran around it. Because of its proximity to these roads, it was worth many times what I paid for it, but it wasn't quiet or ideal for residential living anymore.

I didn't even need to put the land and house up for sale because so many people had been asking about buying it for a long time. With help from Mike Roblyer, I found a young businessman who agreed to give me my asking price and pledged to keep the house that Pearl had designed as an office building, which meant a lot to me.

Annetta and I moved south into the country, away from the congestion and noise of Annapolis. The rural road, large property, and quiet, dark nights made me feel right at home.

Annetta shared the dream that Pearl and I had of using our good fortune for the benefit of the community. We became involved with two projects that we hope would allow our good works to continue after we pass on.

In 2003, with the help of my lawyer, Michael Roblyer, we created the Har-Pearl Foundation. It was to be funded with the money from the sale of my land, which finally took place in 2005. The principal will be invested and the interest will go to churches which set up after-school programs for at-risk students. These programs will provide safe places for these children to play and learn in the hours after school when they might get into trouble. It will take a

Michael Roblyer

Giles Roblyer

while for churches to develop these programs, so, in the meantime, the interest will go to scholarships for needy students to attend colleges such as Morgan State, University of Maryland, University of Maryland Eastern Shore, and my beloved alma mater Hampton University.

The second project involved my farm. Pearl and I had thought about building a dormitory for students and a school for them to attend. In the early 1990s, I obtained a building permit but could not find a group interested in running it. I have been concerned about this project ever since. Annetta had a big dinner at our house for 39 pastors to discuss how we might best use the land. I thought I had found a group that was serious about running a school, and I hired the services of an architect to design the building. Unfortunately, the plans for the project would not work.

I am still looking for a group who can run a successful school on my farm. There must be a source of committed and organized individuals who are dedicated to making a difference for minority students. It would be very satisfying to find a group of honest, knowledgeable, cooperative, and organized people who can carry out the plans that Pearl and I talked about years ago.

I have been honored with several awards for my charity work, but the greatest and most fitting so far is the naming of a college library in honor of Pearl and me. Students will study at the newly constructed Har-Pearl Memorial Library at the Annapolis Southern Maryland Campus of Sojourner-Douglass College. Display cases will highlight some of the Spruill story, and my papers and tributes will be archived in the building. I can't think of a better way to preserve our family's memory than at a college designed for predominantly African-American working adults seeking to earn their college degree or increase their professional knowledge. I feel tremendously honored to be associated in this way with the names of abolitionists and activists Sojourner Truth and Frederick Douglass.

Chapter 12

Looking Back, Looking Ahead

———◆●◆———

Of the nine Spruill children, I am the only one who remains alive. Welton retired from the Norfolk Southern Railways after spending his adult years in Richmond and passed away in October 1993. Carrie, who had provided so much inspiration by getting her teaching degree, died at the age of 89, after a long career in the classroom. Johnson, the diplomat and peacemaker who ran several different schools, died in 1984 at the age of 72. William died in 1980. Elijah, who had played the valuable role of big brother to Al and me, died in 1984. He spent 20 years serving the country in the Navy, which provided a greater education for him about the people and places of the world than any college. My dear sister Von passed in 1999 at the age of 79, after putting her master's degree in education to good use during 42 years as an educator. After a long battle with Alzheimer's, Eva Spruill Pope died in 2005 at the age of 83. She had taught elementary education in Capron, Virginia, for 38 years.

My youngest brother Albert perhaps went the farthest educationally in life of any of the Spruills. He held a bachelor's degree from North Carolina A&T, a master's degree from Iowa State University, and a doctorate in education from Cornell University. He also spent time studying at Stanford and the University of Michigan. He spent 38 years as a lecturer in education and sociology in the school of graduate studies at North Carolina A&T State University. For 23 of those years, he served as Dean of the Graduate School and was passionate about the importance of maintaining and expanding graduate-level education for blacks. He wrote and published constantly throughout his career, including an 18-year run of articles titled "Looking In On Higher Education" for the *Carolina Peacemaker* newspaper. He used this forum to rally people to the righteous cause of desegregation of higher education and equal opportunity for blacks in all facets of the academic world. As for so many of his generation, the struggle for civil rights was just a piece of the larger struggle for human rights. He also followed in our father's footsteps as an ordained deacon in the Baptist Church. He spoke at many of the celebrations in the lives of the Spruill siblings, including my retirement ceremony, and he spoke at many of the funerals of his brothers and sisters. He passed away in 2004 at the age of 78.

Our mother's legacy is the educators who came off the farm in Travis. She transferred to her children the belief in the primacy of education to children, especially those who must rise from an underclass. Our lives were devoted to conveying this message to a much larger world, from my efforts to create a dedicated center for vocational education in Anne Arundel County to Albert's visits to the U.S. Congress to ensure that the highest realms of intellectual pursuits remained open to blacks.

Children don't naturally have knowledge about anything in the adult world. As they grow, they learn from their parents, and that learning process begins with imitation of their mothers and fathers. The true learning process begins slowly. Children should not be expected to make adult decisions at an early age. Instead, structure and discipline are required, and these two qualities were most important to me in teaching. I could talk to the students and they would listen and have respect.

Many children today have parents who do not establish a solid base for their growth. I was fortunate to have two parents who stayed together despite hard times. Minority children have not established good work habits and seem to feel that the world owes them a living, which is not the case. I would like my school and foundation to provide these children with work habits and career skills that they would otherwise not get from their parents or the community. Children coming from the minority underclass must be strong, hard working, and responsible if they are to achieve their goals. They are not born this way, but must be nurtured, guided, and educated if we expect them to find success. The community today provides many leaders but few who are willing to serve as mentors and set examples.

A long life allows one to witness many changes in the world. Race relations are much better than they were when I was a boy, but much remains to be done. I have no doubt that the importance of education has not diminished in the slightest. It is perhaps more important now that so many opportunities are open to children of all races and so few are taught how to take advantage. If I could start over again today, I would still choose to be an educator. I think the other Spruill children would feel the same way.

In addition to education, minority ownership of land and business is the way forward. These goals, however, cannot be accomplished without serious long-term planning and sacrifice. The path to ownership and wealth that can be used to help the younger generations is not easy, but it is vital to their future.

My siblings and I journeyed a long way from that small farm in Travis. At the end of our lives, we can be proud to leave behind a legacy of service and learning.

I hope others will follow our path and find their own ways to better themselves and their community.

I believe that when children come into this world, they know nothing and are helpless. They depend upon their parents or caretakers for guidance. Some are easy to rear and others are not. To think that a child that has never experienced food for instance, how can they decide or pick their own cereal or other foods other than their parent's habits or caretakers? They cannot decide. Usually today's children have seen most of these things on television or on the Internet. Parents or caretakers have the responsibility to train them in eating the correct foods or wearing the proper attire. I am not talking from theory, but experience. My own children never wanted to eat breakfast and I knew that breakfast was an important meal. I made them get up and eat breakfast before they were off to school. Sometimes their limited experience will cause them to feel that they are being neglected. For instance, my two children because I put so much emphasis on work and wanted them to follow my example. Lots of time they would resist. Sometimes they accuse me of working too much and not paying enough attention to them. In growing up, I used to take home movies of family activities and I produce the many movies that I had produce and put them together; they could not ignore that I spent lots of time with them while growing up. I always put lots of time pushing education in my family. My son used to resist even though he had a score of almost 1400 on the SAT Test. I did not change my mind. He had to get an education and he was to stay at my house.

I am not ashamed that I made him attend two colleges even though he was grown. He had to go if he stayed at my house. I paid all the expenses but I am sure it has paid off even though he has never told me so. I feel that I have done the right thing. I would do it all over again. I have no second thoughts about it.

Larry Crow, who has a high position at Smith, Rawlings, let me know that I gave him good guidance at that stage of his life. He was one of my students at the Shaw Shop, on Chinquapin Round Road. He also said

Larry Crow and his son, R. C. Crow.

101

that I saved him from going off and getting in trouble. Dave White, another student, has a shop on Chinquapin Round Road. He thanked me for teaching the trade of body and fender repair enough to open an excellent body shop. I felt very proud of these students and feel that my patience has helped me to be able to influence the student's lives.

Dave White

This is a letter from parents of some former students:

Dear Mr. Spruill,

We would like to take this opportunity to express our gratitude to you for all you have done. You have taught three of our sons and they all have the deepest respect for you. Especially thank you for the guidance you gave Eddie that led to his final accomplishments.

With deepest respect and gratitude,

Rhodice & Jakie Housley

Harold "Jakie" and Rose Marie "Rhodie" Housley

Harold Housley, Jr.
1968

Lester Housley
1972

George "Eddie" Housley
1989

In keeping with the type of person I am which is to plan 5 to 10 years ahead, I bought property in Tracy's Landing five years ago with the plans to move into the house later. The land is located one mile from my farm. The idea was to rent the house out for a few years and sell my property in Annapolis and move further in the country. This is the third house I have lived in since 1962. I am not of the generation that moves a lot. I settle in one place but when I was living in Annapolis every house I would build; a county or state road would either take my house or come close and this was the case of my property in the Annapolis area.

I had been living on Womack Drive for 18 years and felt that I would live the rest of my life there. Things changed in that area and companies began to build around me and roads came close to my house; so I felt that I could not keep my family there. I did not have to put my house and land up for sale, because of the location. I had many people asking about buying it. It almost went into a bidding war, but I refuse to let that happen. So a young businessman agreed to give me my asking price. He was the only one that said he would keep the house as an office building and would not tear it down. That impressed me.

Epilogue

———◆●◆———

We must have more programs to help our youth. I believe that goal setting and a strong work ethic is paramount to the success of adult individuals as they work to help our society to serve the needs of all. Young children need to develop appropriate attitudes about work and also about community involvement. Hard work and a focus program certainly keeps one on track who is trying to meet success. A strong program that is similar to the Arlington Echo Center in Millersville, MD will help keep the idle mind busy for the right reasons. It is said, "an idle mind is the Devil's workshop."

Dr. Charlestine Fairley, Director of Sojourner-Douglass College, Annapolis Southern Maryland Campus visited the Spruill Farm and marveled at the potential that the farm could offer to young children and adults. There are many wonderful learning strategies that can be taught through a farm project. Children can be taught to share, to build a garden and to observe the growing of plants from seed to harvest. They can also be taught how to care for plants and how the same technique for growing plants can transfer to the nature and care of people.

After many weeks and months of collaboration with Sojourner-Douglass College, I decided to transfer my farmland that covers many acres, to the Sojourner-Douglass College Annapolis Southern Maryland Campus. The College will receive a renovated barn and a new education building on the site. We hope that someday the farm project will involve classes from the public schools as well as adult groups that will be able to hold retreats and other productive gatherings there. With the vision of

Dr. Fairley and other Sojourner-Douglass College associates, I am convinced that my ideas about education on the farm will be realized.

I wondered what would happen to our plans for a program especially since the death of my wife Pearl. She did not live long enough to enjoy the rapid progress made by the organizations and groups that Pearl and I had been working with. Now that she is deceased, it is up to me to carry on. As I tried to interest other groups in planning education programs at the farm, I never seemed to peek their interest.

One evening during the winter of 2005, Dr. Eleanor M. Harris called me to talk about all of the support that I have contributed to the community over many years. She asked to meet with me to discuss a recommendation that she wanted to make to Sojourner-Douglass College, stating that she needed my consent to do so. I agreed to meet with her on the following Sunday afternoon. By the time she arrived at my home, and following some brief discussion, I was amazed by what she shared and how agreeable it was to me. She continued to share how Pearl and I opened our home to community groups and worked diligently at my church – First Baptist Church of Annapolis – to establish programs for youth of the church and community. All of this effort had gone unnoticed and Dr. Harris wanted to recommend my name for recognition during the grand opening of the new Sojourner-Douglass College Southern Maryland Campus, in Edgewater, Maryland.

We met a few times and I later agreed that my name could be submitted for recognition. We also discussed the need to recognize the great work that Pearl and I had done many years ago. I finally shared with Dr. Harris that I had established a foundation and named it the Har-Pearl Foundation to help provide education support to those anxious to attend school but had only limited resources. We talked about the new Sojourner-Douglass College building and the need for funds to support the library, bookstore and other aspects of the College. We agreed that the library is a vital part of learning and acquiring skills necessary for success and I agreed to help fund it. I suggested that if we name the library the Har-Pearl Memorial Library I would make substantial financial contributions to the College. I thought this would be a wonderful way to honor Pearl because she had worked so long and hard for many years.

Dr. Harris helped change my mind because I had been disappointed for so many years and was hesitant about what she indicated could happen for me. Truly, I wondered if these things that we discussed would ever happen. Finally, I decided to allow Dr. Harris to recommend my name to the College as a supporter of education programs especially in Anne Arundel County.

Following the Honorary Luncheon named in my honor with Dr. Dorothy I. Height as Honorary Chairperson of the event, and a wonderful greeting from the President of Sojourner-Douglass College, Dr. Charles W. Simmons, I was ecstatic about everything. The College refers to me as a "Philanthropist and a Just Man who walks in his integrity." The foresight and vision of Dr. Charlestine Fairley will always be etched in my view of the College. That is why I am supporting the wonderful work of the school. I believe they will make great strides in working to bring the farm project to a level that will keep delivering educational services to the youth and adults in the community.

Acknowledgements

I offer my warmest appreciation to the many supporter who have assisted me in this effort to complete my memoirs.

To **Michael Roblyer**, for the faith he had in me at a time when I had many doubts.

He accompanied me to South County meetings and stayed there with me through out the discussions I had with farm neighbors.

My gratitude to **Giles Roblyer** who took on the task of helping me as I began to write my book. His involvement is especially endearing since I had at least four other people over a period of five years who received money from me and never delivered a written manuscript.

To **Dr. Eleanor Harris** for her kind words during my retirement banquet at the Bay Ridge Inn where she presented me with the retirement recognition from the Anne Arundel County Board of Education. Dr. Harris was instrumental in getting me involved with Sojourner-Douglass College that so graciously honored me in 2005.

I am extremely pleased to have met **Dr. Charlestine Fairley** a visionary with the ability to recognize my farm ideas as a positive project for the community. It is a pleasure working with her and the school to bring the farm operations to reality. My gratitude to her and Sojourner-Douglass College for partnering with me.

To **Pearl Spruill** who kept me focused on programs for the young people in the community and for the many hours she contributed to selling our farm vegetables to raise funds to support programs for children in the Annapolis area.

To **Aris T. Allen Jr.** who has worked with me for many years on a variety of building projects at my former residence at 2 Womack Drive in Parole and he continues to assist me at the Tracy's Landing location where I now reside and at the farm location where he is designing the educational center to be built by me and used by Sojourner-Douglass College. I am fortunate to have this young man who demonstrates a commitment to my ideas and assists me in bringing those ideas to reality.

To **Dr. Donald C. Roane** who is an inspiration to me. He has shared his time and expertise in helping me to establish The Har-Pearl Foundation that will help countless members of the community including Sojourner-Douglass College.

To **Minister and Mrs. Richard McClain** for their steadfast and relentless efforts to keep my computer operational as we worked to complete the manuscript. Their support has been absolutely timeless as they worked to help us use the computer for processing various stages of the manuscript.

Many thanks to **Wallace Williams** for the genuine manner in which he has worked as the manager of the farm project for the youth at First Baptist Church in Annapolis Maryland. I know that there were times when he felt like giving up, but he never did. Under his leadership, we operated three vegetable stands at the County's Farmers Markets in three different locations. The money raised from the sales was used to purchase computers for the church. Wallace Williams made certain that children were a part of the selling process.

Mary Ann Taliaferro, for your invaluable help as a

consultant and accountant in processing the necessary information for monetary contributions and expenses. I couldn't have done it owithout your expertise.

William Snowden Keys a member of my fraternity assisted with the farm project when the fraternity helped at the market and on the farm picking vegetables to be carried to the market for sale. He gave me books for the proposed new education center and I am most apprecia- tive of his gesture of support.

My gratitude to **Robert Brooks** for his hard work and perseverance. When the fraternity helped me with the farm project, he delivered the produce to the farmers market at his own expense. All of the funds made at that time went to the fraternity's treasury to be used for schol- arships and youth programs. He is a tireless worker who to this day continues to assist me at the farm.

My wonderful friend **John Prann** who was my co- worker at Wiley H. Bates High School and will always be remembered for loaning me the funds to purchase my first garage for working on cars and also for helping me with the purchase of the land that I owned in Parole. He is the man that got me started toward the success that I now enjoy. Although he is deceased, I am still reminded of his goodness.

I am honored to have had my Church family in Annapolis work with me to do so many things to help the youth and uplift humanity in Annapolis and in Anne Arundel County.

Earl Jones, a former student, has worked with me as an adult for many years. It has been a pleasure observing lessons taught to him come to light through his work with me on the farm. I am very proud of his loyalty and com- mitment to me and the farm that I cherish.

To **Steve Pope** – thank you for finding my mother's picture among the family heirlooms.

To my brother-in-law, **Anthony Jordan**, my sisters, **Vonbeulah** and **Margo** for sending me such marvelous pictures of my hometown in North Carolina...
Thank you.
To my son, **Kevin**, and my daughter, **Kecia**, I am delighted to have enjoyed the opportunity to exhibit the father image to them as children and now as they continue to demonstrate my teachings as they enjoy adulthood. My grandchildren **Jazlyn**, **Myles**, and **Sarah** are also an inspiration to me.

My hope is that my stepson, **Jay Pittman**, son, **Kevin Spruill**, and daughter, **Kecia Y. Johnson**, will benefit from this book as a visionary path to the future for their lives in society. They are hardworking young people and indeed, with consistency in their work, much success is waiting for them. Kecia, Jay and Kevin are great writers and maybe one day we will receive a book from them. My son Kevin is also a graphic artist and loves his work. Hopefully, reading my book will give them a spark of light to enter into the world as writers and business people.

Last but not least, I am humbled by the great work, time and care of my loving wife **Annetta**, who stands by me in all that I do on the farm, at church, in the community and at home. As an educator, she has helped me by proofing, typing, collecting pictures and doing all of the leg work necessary to get this book ready for the publisher. In addition, her support to all of the programs that I have attempted to put in place have her stamp of approval. I am blessed for having her in my life.

ISBN 141208199-8